THE ART OF HARD CONVERSATIONS

"Bam! Lori Roeleveld does it again . . . and again . . . and again! She lures you in with her words and leads you straight to the One who is the ultimate answer to every hard conversation. Her books come alive and have a way of connecting our mind with our heart. *The Art of Hard Conversations* helps us to proceed with caution yet maintain our perspective. When we must engage in hard conversations, Lori shows us how to do it with love. Which, after all, is what life is really about."

Tammy Whitehurst, motivational speaker, author, and co-owner of
Christian Communicators Conference

"Real, practical advice on the art of leaning into hard conversations. Roeleveld offers compassion, insight, and guidance to help us speak the truth in love. A book all of us need."

Tosca Lee, *New York Times* best-selling author

"In *The Art of Hard Conversations*, Lori Roeleveld beautifully avoids preaching by telling her own story—what she's learned, how she's changed, and the dramatic difference it's made in her life. That's the kind of message that reaches me, and it'll reach you too."

Jerry B. Jenkins, author of the Left Behind series and
writing coach

"As someone skilled at conflict avoidance (that's a nice way of saying I'm terrified of confrontation), I picked up *The Art of Hard Conversations* prepared to be challenged to grow a spine and scrounge up some courage. What I discovered in these pages was a conversation—at times humorous, at times poignant, always deeply personal and transparent. Lori writes like a friend who understands my fears and struggles and doesn't want to change my personality but wants to equip me within the framework of my own God-given design. As a coach and confidant, Lori gently encourages both the bold and the bashful to approach hard conversations with finesse and grace. *The Art of Hard Conversations* is a resource I will be returning to again and again."

Lynn H. Blackburn, best-selling and award-winning author of
Beneath the Surface and *In Too Deep*

"Once again Lori Stanley Roeleveld speaks straight to your soul. Each lesson lingers in your heart as she encourages and empowers you to trust your instincts and your heavenly Father in the delicate art of difficult conversations with those you love. This is a must-read for every parent, child, spouse, and friend."

Bethany Jett, award-winning author of *The Cinderella Rule*

"Why should we invest ourselves in hard conversations, in encounters that seem so likely to go wrong, to cause even more pain, to be a waste of time? 'They are hard because they matter' is Lori's deep conviction, and in this highly readable book, she proves this point that many of us miss, while unveiling practical strategies that equip everyone for the inevitable difficulties and drama. This is clear, strong, gently confrontational writing that lets no one off the hook and yet affirms everyone's potential for breakthroughs inside us and between us. Lori's message is life-giving, liberating, and bracing, fortifying us to face conflict and estrangement, as well as our own fears and insecurities. With an obvious concern for our emotional health and interpersonal integrity, Lori invites us to explore God's Word as the guide for selecting our words, and to submit ourselves to God's Spirit, who reshapes our character and refines our speech. I enthusiastically recommend this book for people of all ages and backgrounds, for all of us who feel at a loss in stressful verbal interactions."

Doug Stevens, pastor of Community Covenant Church, Lenexa, Kansas

"Lori has written an excellent manual for talking to others about challenging topics with the foundation of knowing Christ. I was encouraged to trust the Word and the Holy Spirit, who gives discernment and leads us as well as those we must talk to, to see clearly what is in our own hearts. She lifts up the truth of our Redeemer so we can grasp how much freedom there is in trusting His ways of humility and kindness, rather than our own ideas of how someone must be 'fixed.' I love this book and highly recommend it to anyone longing to have good, kind, and genuinely helpful conversations!"

Valerie Elliot Shepard, author of *Devotedly* and daughter of Elisabeth Elliot

THE ART OF
HARD
Biblical Tools
for the Tough Talks
That Matter
CONVERSATIONS

LORI STANLEY ROELEVELD

Kregel
Publications

The Art of Hard Conversations: Biblical Tools for the Tough Talks That Matter
© 2019 by Lori Stanley Roeleveld

Published by Kregel Publications, a division of Kregel Inc., 2450 Oak Industrial Dr. NE, Grand Rapids, MI 49505.

Names and personal identifiers (except for immediate family members of the author) have been changed to honor privacy concerns.

Scripture quotations are from The Holy Bible, English Standard Version® (ESV®), copyright © 2001 by Crossway, a publishing ministry of Good News Publishers. Used by permission. All rights reserved.

Cover photo by Jack Finnigan on Unsplash

ISBN 978-0-8254-4555-2, print
ISBN 978-0-8254-7526-9, epub

Printed in the United States of America
19 20 21 22 23 24 25 26 27 28 / 5 4 3 2 1

Dedicated to Rev. Doug Stevens
You were pivotal in inciting me to live radically for Jesus,
to root my soul in biblical truth, and to seek from God the
courage to write light into a dark world. Nothing to prove
and nothing to lose—all the way home, my brother.

CONTENTS

FOREWORD

If there was only one word to describe my social abilities, it would be *zilch*. For me, navigating a conversation is just as hard as navigating traffic, and I have no sense of direction when it comes to doing either. Which explains how I ended up making a wrong turn and driving to Alaska, where I lived as a hermit in a remote cabin for five years.

At that point in my life I had decided that I'd much rather engage an angry grizzly in a conversation than another human being. At least then I stood a better chance of escaping unscathed. That remote Alaskan cabin is where I met Jesus, though, and where I felt my call to use my talents to write and minister in the entertainment industry, which meant returning to the Lower 48 and facing my biggest fear . . . people.

Although my life changed in Alaska, my social awkwardness remained unaffected. Whenever I faced a difficult conversation, I found myself stammering and flailing to look for the right words—the way a drowning person looks for a life vest.

And that's exactly what *The Art of Hard Conversations* has become to me. It's a life vest for the conversationally challenged, and an essential tool to consult during those times when you feel like you're struggling to stay afloat amid the sometimes choppy waters of relationships.

I had the opportunity to put some of Lori's tools to the test when I encountered a stranger crying at a highway rest area. Having committed some of Lori's advice to memory, I had the confidence to start a hard conversation, and God supplied the rest of the words I needed as we talked. I was able to overcome the awkwardness and to comfort a grieving heart with the knowledge that God cares.

Lori has packed this book with God's Word, her own life lessons, profound wisdom, and numerous tips and techniques that will keep your head above water and your spirit flowing in the right direction. I'd recommend it to anyone who struggles when it comes to finding the right words for a difficult conversation. I'm sending copies of this book to several family members—and to a couple of grizzlies with anger issues.

Torry Martin
Actor, Author, Screenwriter

ACKNOWLEDGMENTS

My deepest thanks to:

Dennis Hillman, Steve Barclift, Janyre Tromp, Elizabeth Smith, Noelle Pedersen, Joel Armstrong, and the entire team at Kregel Publications for your craftsmanship, creativity, and insight.

Les Stobbe for bringing me up in this work of writing for God, and Bob Hostetler for taking me on for the next chapter.

The Light Brigade, the First Baptist Church of Hope Valley, and my prayer team for making this book happen. The Art of Hard Conversations Facebook group for your frank feedback.

Rubart for the kick in the pants. Kathy for always listening. Torry for your strong encouragement. Professor Brian Eck for teaching me to look for the image of God in every person.

Rob, my kids, grandkids, and parents for pulling together through the hardest year of our lives and encouraging me to keep writing through it all.

Why Bother Having Hard Conversations? (Why Is It an Art?)

Your next conversation could impact someone's life forever. Maybe you've been delaying it, or until now, you've talked without effect. This book will guide you toward fruitful dialogue that will make a difference—possibly for eternity.

Like most things in life, conversations that present the greatest challenge also provide the biggest reward. The keys to transformation, unification, and authentic breakthroughs are usually found on the other side of hard conversations.

If you pay attention to the way God works, you won't be surprised when I suggest most soul-shaping, life-altering discussions will happen not before international audiences or from televised pulpits but in kitchens, cubicles, and foyers and on front porches. Much like shepherds locating the King of Kings in a smelly stable, seemingly inconsequential settings can provide the backdrop for exchanges that convert coffee shop booths into outposts of glory.

▎ Hard conversations are hard because they matter.

You may be the only one who can make this happen for the people (or person) you had in mind when you opened this book. They don't realize it, but on some level, they're depending on you to get this right. Whether you're a hesitant conversationalist or an enthusiastic but blundering one, the tools here will equip you for rapid and lasting improvement when connecting with others using the common vehicle of conversation. Like other ordinary things—bread, water, wine—conversation is elevated to new heights and deeper meanings at the touch of our Lord.

You're not alone. We all look for help on this topic. Hard conversations are hard because they matter. When subjects are important, we can let their magnitude either paralyze us into avoidance or push us into premature, often clumsy efforts.

Like our Father God, we seek to communicate. Often, the ideas we want to convey have eternal ramifications. But when we do try to speak on weighty topics, discuss deeply personal issues, or explain our perspective to someone who differs, it can be challenging to get out of our own way. We want our words to flow unimpeded, but too often, they crash, causing conversational traffic jams. Our intent gets lost in the clamor of verbal horns honking and emotional sirens blaring.

While hard conversations are difficult, they're also inevitable, necessary, and often, biblically imperative. Speaking tough truths and comforting people through trials are expected undertakings for Jesus followers. But too often, we either fumble or flee. And there is no scientific formula to successful hard conversations. Because of this, I believe the subject merits an entire book.

▌Barriers arise around tough talks because our enemy knows they're a spiritual front line.

After decades of study and practice, I've come to view hard conversations as an art—usually a language art, often a healing art, sometimes a performing art, and occasionally a martial art.

They are obviously a language art because they involve words. A healing art, because through them, we open doors for God to heal hearts, minds, souls, and relationships—often in ways we cannot imagine. They are like a performing art because there's significant commitment and practice required (sometimes for years) involving flubs and follies, to produce a work of beauty and awe. And there are others behind the scenes (coaching, praying, and so forth) contributing to any success.

Hard conversations are like a martial art. They are key instruments of deepening relationships, resolving conflicts, encouraging spiritual growth, and spreading the gospel, and the evil one would rather we avoid them in fear instead of facing them in faith.

Barriers arise around tough talks because our enemy knows they're a spiritual front line. Countless people are damaged by situations or conditions that might have been avoided if someone had been willing to have a hard conversation early on.

I believe hard conversations are also a sacred art, a calling by Christ on our lives, a kingdom-building work He compels us and equips us to do. Speaking truth is one way we invoke Jesus in our everyday and represent Him even in common moments.

Like me, you want to follow Jesus, even into hard conversations. Your love for God and for others is prodding you to release your hold on the comfort of silence or relinquish the habit of saying too much too fast. You want your words to make a difference, but you're worried you don't have what it takes. You do.

I wrote this book with just you in mind. I've designed it for readers who want to have effective, fruitful conversations, even when that's hard. We'll discuss spiritual principles and specific strategies anyone can employ to improve challenging conversations. I'll share some of my biggest failures and you can learn from what I've done wrong, as well as what I've learned to do right.

As with any art, one may initially learn about it through reading or hearing, but at some point, we must interact with and practice the skills ourselves. I strongly urge you to employ the tools in the ARTwork exercises following each lesson. There are three to five lessons within each unit, fewer lessons when there are more skills to practice. We change best in small bites, so Answering a thought question, Reading relevant Scripture, and Trying a new conversational tool (hence ARTwork) will serve you in improving your ability to talk about hard things.

You'll find I've included many examples and stories, from both biblical passages and modern-life situations. In some, you'll identify with the initiator of the chat. In others, you'll relate to the participant. There's something to learn from each. This isn't a book about good guys and bad guys, "goofuses and gallants." It's about complex, faulted, hopeful humans trying to connect through conversations, even when it's hard, over subjects that matter.

We'll cover the personalities and styles we bring to conversations. I'll explain some of the internal walls we must either dismantle, descend, or dismiss for more productive exchanges. I'll provide a six-question soul preparation that will better equip you to initiate talks. We'll cover the heart-work we must do to prepare and the hard work of navigating conversations with loved ones about trials, with strangers about salvation, and with friends about faith. These skills will serve us whether we initiate the talks or they are thrust upon us.

Additionally, you'll benefit from employing the assignments, Bible readings, and tips I've included at the end of each unit. These little "Heart of the Art Practice" sections afford you even more opportunity to grow in your new skills.

We follow a God who calls us into relationship. We're to demonstrate biblical living. That means obedience and action, but it also means that sometimes we must open our mouths and let words come out. We want those words to reach their mark.

Studying the Scriptures referenced in this book, practicing the strategies, and enlisting the ongoing support of other mature believers will set you on the road of working alongside Jesus in this ministry of hard conversations.

It won't happen overnight. Every sacred art takes time, practice, and the work of the Holy Spirit. We won't perfect it until we're all home, but we can certainly make an adventure of trying.

Colossians 1:28–29 says this: "Him we proclaim, warning everyone and teaching everyone with all wisdom, that we may present everyone mature in Christ. For this I toil, struggling with all his energy that he powerfully works within me." As we obey the call of this verse, we will encounter enough hard conversations to last a lifetime, so we best be prepared.

Exhale. Be hopeful in Christ. Let's begin.

PART 1

Perspectives and Personalities—Understanding and Embracing the Challenge

The Place of Personality in Hard Conversations

Lesson 1

The Life You Save May Be Your Own

Moreover, he said to me, "Son of man, all my
words that I shall speak to you receive in your
heart, and hear with your ears. And go to the
exiles, to your people, and speak to them and
say to them, 'Thus says the Lord GOD,' whether
they hear or refuse to hear." (Ezek. 3:10–11)

I was ten when I stood beside my dad's recliner and told him he was in a coma. That was the first hard conversation that changed my life.

Dad was a wall of inattention in my childhood. As a volunteer fire chief with a day job, if he wasn't working, he was fighting fires. He wasn't home often, but when he was, it was usually after a stop by the local bar to decompress. Our lives were messy back then.

I was desperate to reach him. Like every child does, I craved a full relationship with my father. I longed for his attention, but by ten, apparently I'd realized it wasn't going to happen soon. So, I navigated the problem in a way that worked for me and then gathered my nerve to inform him. Since I was only encouraged to speak during commercials, I'd rehearsed saying what I had to say quickly.

"Dad, from now on, I'm going to treat you like you're in a coma. I believe the dad I need is in there somewhere and can hear me. Even if you can't show me that you love me, I know you do. So, I'm just going to talk to you when I feel like it. You can respond whenever you're ready. One day you'll decide to come out of your coma. This way, when you do, we'll have already been having these kinds of chats. Okay, well, that's all. I love you."

He didn't even acknowledge I'd spoken. Not then. But one day, when I was in my late twenties, my dad did, in fact, "wake up" to the relationships in his immediate circle. For the later decades of his life we've been very close. Our family has had the joy of knowing him as a changed man, through the power of prayer and the grace of Jesus.

It took a lot for me, as a child, to speak those words. They had no visible effect on him, but they freed me. In a powerful way, his inability to carry on his end of the conversation no longer held me hostage. It's a freedom I believe more of us can experience.

The awesome beauty and terrifying truth of hard conversations is that even if the outcome isn't what we had hoped, they still have the power to set at least one of the participants free. And our job isn't to change someone. Our job is to speak "whether they hear or refuse to hear."

Hard conversations free us either to work toward resolution or to walk away without regret.

We should always aim for true dialogue. Plan for mutual breakthrough. Plant our faith firmly on Jesus's ability to redeem any situation, relationship, or individual. But when the other person chooses to remain on the other side of the wall, we can still experience release. Hard conversations free us either to work toward resolution or to walk away without regret.

When I was still too young to appreciate the dynamic of it, God led me into a conversation with Dad that freed me in a way I wouldn't understand for many years. He didn't change, so I changed. More than that, I named the problem, created boundaries I could live within, and informed him of my choice to write a different story than we were currently living.

Yes, I was a child, but I was a child who knew Jesus, and that made all the difference.

Hard conversations challenge everyone. We avoid them to our detriment or abuse them to our harm. Most of us resist bringing up uncomfortable topics, and all of us squirm when others initiate such conversations with us.

We encounter hard conversations with family, within the church, and with people who don't follow Jesus. They pop up everywhere, and most days, we feel ill-equipped to navigate sensitive subjects the way we truly wish we could. What if we could address those challenges and find ways to have more real conversations about hard things? We can.

As I said in the introduction, hard conversations are hard because they matter. We can let their difficulty deter us or determine us. But Christians do hard things every day, by the power of Jesus Christ. Why should navigating meaningful conversations be any different, especially when we know they can be vehicles for freedom? If a ten-year-old girl can find courage in Christ to speak truth to a disaffected father, we can *all* take heart that Jesus provides what we need to tackle the tough topics in our lives.

ARTwork

Answer: What were some hard conversations you experienced in childhood? What was the outcome?

Read: God commands us to speak up but holds our listeners responsible for their reaction. What light does Ezekiel 3:10–11 shed on this idea? How can understanding that free us to initiate conversations?

Try: Reframe. I didn't know I was doing it (and I don't recommend telling people they're in a coma), but what God helped me do in childhood was reframe my relationship with my father. Dad's inattention made me feel unloved, but I knew the truth was that he did love me. I chose to live and act in that truth.

We interact daily with people who reject biblical truth, so many of our hard conversations will benefit from reframing.

To reframe, we simply state without judgment what we have observed to be the other person's understanding of the truth. Then clearly say our understanding of truth and explain how that truth informs our actions.

Example: "You've decided to live together without getting married because in our culture, it's become acceptable and seemingly without consequence. You obviously love each other and believe your decision doesn't hurt anyone. It's my perspective that even though many of us do it imperfectly, marriage is sacred. It's my understanding that no matter how it appears, it's better to obey rather than to disobey God. There can be unforeseen consequences from choosing to oppose God's ways. Because of that and the fact that I care about you, I continue to urge you to choose marriage."

Or "You're sad right now and feel like that feeling will never go away. You've been through a lot of hard times and losses, so that's understandable. The truth is, those trials have changed you and altered your life, but you won't always feel this sad, and there are even times of joy ahead of you. Everyone has hardships to endure, but they do end. There is more. And even though you feel as if Jesus has lost sight of you, He hasn't. He isn't done writing your story."

Lesson 2

Swooping Hawks

*Is it by your understanding that the hawk soars
and spreads his wings toward the south?
(Job 39:26)*

Regardless of personality or age, we all would prefer to operate from within our comfort zone, but obedience leads us into uncomfortable territory. Some of us tend to be bold, strong hawks ready to swoop in and carry a conversation on the mighty wings of our opinions and forceful arguments. Others of us, like retreating turtles, prefer to keep our heads down, nestled into our comfortable shells. Still others resemble camouflaged chameleons, switching back and forth between advance and retreat depending on circumstances.

While each tendency has its strengths, they all have weaknesses. We face tough decisions about obeying Jesus despite our lesser tendencies if we love God and want to follow Him into this kingdom adventure. Right now, we'll look at three different types of typical communication styles—along with how God calls us to communicate. First, the swooping hawk.

For the more zealous among us, it can be challenging to exercise restraint rather than dominate conversations and hope an abundance of words will sway hearts. While there are limits to any analogy, it's helpful to imagine that some of us lean toward being conversational hawks.

Some of us spend decades learning to slow down to the speed of Light.

It's a thing of beauty to watch a hawk swoop toward prey, unless you're the prey. Hawks are swift, but while speed is expedient, it's seldom inspired when it comes to hard conversations. We've all heard of flash conversions, but heart transformation generally requires a sizable investment of time. Some of us spend decades learning to slow down to the speed of Light.

Consider the apostle Peter in Matthew 16:22 trying to dissuade Jesus from prophesying his own suffering, or in John 13 resisting Jesus's footwashing and insisting he would lay down his life for Him. Peter's passion often drove his words. Some of us hawks see ourselves in Peter or in this sister in Christ who once invited me for coffee. I sat across from the woman who'd invited me out (why is it always over coffee?), cupping my mug with both hands, so she wouldn't notice them shaking. "I'm not sure I understand what you want from me," I said.

Her tone indicated this shouldn't be hard to understand. "As I explained, several of us have noticed you crying in church. It's really affecting our experience of worship," she replied.

I glanced around the coffee shop to see if anyone could overhear. "I've had a lot of stress recently. My kids are little, and my husband travels so much."

She nodded. "And so, you see, that's why we think you should take a break from being involved in ministry."

"Because I've cried during worship?"

"Well, yes, and so that you can tend to your marriage. It clearly needs tending."

"But Rob's gone most of the time."

"Exactly."

"Help me understand. You've noticed my distress, and it bothers you. So, your solution is that I step down and stay home to take better care of a man who isn't there?"

She nodded, seeming relieved that I finally understood.

I attempted, again, to explain how I felt. "But I especially look forward to interacting with adults during those ministry opportunities. And it's not likely to change the demands of my husband's job for me to be home more often."

"I had a feeling you'd be difficult. Your stubborn attitude and lack of concern about how you're affecting the rest of us indicates to me this is a spiritual issue. Even more reason you shouldn't be in any position right now. I'll discuss this with the team tonight. I was hoping to avoid the discomfort of that. I do hate that you've forced me to take it to that level."

I apologized for being so much trouble.

Though perhaps not evident here, this woman has a real heart for ministering to Christian women. I believe she loves God and wants to serve others, but she's slow to listen and quick to offer solutions (the opposite of James 1:19–20).

At the time, I was a young wife and mother. Yes, I was struggling, but I was also indulging in self-pity. If I'd felt heard or loved during that conversation, we may have reached a solution together.

It's embarrassing to admit, but at times, I've been both women in this conversation. Here, I was the victim, but at other times, I've swooped in with my agenda, ignoring others' hearts and needs. Maybe you can relate, but seriously, I find removing the log from my own eye a relentless process (Matt. 7:3–5).

There's a place for the swift swoop of a hawk in Christlike conversations, but we're called to be praying people, not preying ones.

ARTwork

Answer: What are the advantages and disadvantages of having a hawk conversational style? How is it a benefit to the work of furthering the kingdom, and when might it detract from the work?

Read: Consider Peter's declarations in John 13, particularly verses 6–9 and 36–37. How does Jesus respond to Peter? What encouragement can we hawks take from that? What caution?

Try: Listen as others converse around you today (if you're confined to home, try this watching a talk show or movie). Note how others respond to the hawk conversational style. If they were your friends, how might you encourage them?

Lesson 3

Retreating Turtles

*But he said, "Oh, my Lord, please send
someone else." (Exod. 4:13)*

I was on staff at a local gym when I walked into our workout room to find one of our regulars sobbing on a moving treadmill. She was a lovely, older woman. Off the treadmill, she relied on a cane, which leaned against the rail. Concerned with her heart and her safety, I hurried over to ask what was wrong.

She shook her head, crying. "I just read one of your blogs."

Panic. I was new to blogging, and word of it had spread through the gym. Most of the regulars weren't Christians, so I forewarned them it was unapologetically a "Jesus" blog, but many couldn't resist a curious peek. "I'm sorry it upset you. What can I do to help?"

She sobbed even more. "Can I know Jesus? Can I get to know Him like you do?"

I panicked. Silently, I prayed, "Jesus, you know I'm a remedial evangelist. This isn't a proper starting point for a rookie." Do you ever counsel Jesus? I strongly advise against it. "It doesn't even seem safe to accept Jesus on a moving treadmill. There must be some other Christian—*any* other Christian—who would be better in this moment than I am. Couldn't you send one here now?"

Not a prayer I recall with pride.

The gym teemed with onlookers. Conversation bubbles appeared over their heads (I may have imagined this part). They read, "Wow. How's she going to handle this?" or "She's not seriously going to pray with this woman right here, is she?"

I wish I could say I mustered my nerve and boldly led this woman to Jesus despite the bizarre circumstances, but the truth is, I couldn't locate my voice. In that moment, I embodied the Corinthians' complaint about the apostle Paul: "For they say, 'His letters are weighty and strong, but his bodily presence is weak, and his speech of no account'" (2 Cor. 10:10).

I stopped the treadmill, escorted her to a chair, and quietly provided instructions as to how to follow Jesus. I stopped just shy of anything resembling an invitation to pray there and then. I fell short of that opportunity.

God extended me an invitation to participate in advancing His kingdom, but I hesitated and withdrew into my shell. When presented with the moment, I couldn't imagine I was the right person for the task, despite God's clear indication that I was. I missed out. When our hesitation overrides God's invitation, we opt out of opportunities to shadow our Father in His work.

> **God leads us into situations and conversations knowing full well our limitations, but He never leaves us without help.**

God leads us into situations and conversations knowing full well our limitations, but He never leaves us without help. Moses clearly had turtle tendencies and yet God chose him to confront Pharaoh and to demand he set the Israelites free. God provided Moses with a staff for courage and Aaron for support. He may call some of us turtles on similarly challenging tasks, but He will provide us what we need as well.

God is eager to include us in the work of furthering His kingdom, guiding Christians into deeper relationship with Him, encouraging and exhorting others to spiritual maturity, and ministering to people in their darkest moments. For our Father, it's always take your son and daughter to work day.

God created a variety of temperaments, some more reserved than others, and we should rejoice in that. If you're reserved or given to few words, embrace God's design. But none of us should use our design as an excuse to avoid engaging in kingdom work. God created turtles with shells, but we can stick our necks out, as easily as we can retract them.

ARTwork

Answer: What are the advantages and disadvantages of having a turtle conversational style? How is it a benefit to the work of furthering the kingdom, and when might it detract from the work?

Read: Read about Moses's struggle in Exodus 4:1–17. What about this conversation surprises you? What comfort can we turtles take from God's response to Moses? What warning?

Try: Listen to conversations around you again today, but this time, pay attention to those who are speaking less than others. What can you tell from observing turtles? How do people respond to them? If they were your friends, how might you encourage them?

Lesson 4

Camouflaged Chameleons

I have become all things to all people, that by
all means I might save some. (1 Cor. 9:22)

The lunch crowd at my old office was an opinionated bunch. I found it intimidating and appreciated that one of the other staff also seemed to remain quiet during what could be heated debates on headlines. I saw another side of this staffer one day, though, when someone wondered aloud, "What kinds of people would sink to relying on government programs for food and shelter?"

"I'm 'those kinds of people,'" she said quietly but firmly.

"Excuse me?" someone asked, as everyone looked her way.

"I said that I'm one of 'those kinds of people.' Some of us have no one to fall back on. After my husband left, I had to consider my kids, not my pride. Tom, didn't you and your wife move in with your parents this year? And, Julia, your father cosigned for your car. I don't have help, so I rely on a government program. I don't know what kind of person that makes me, but here I am, having lunch with all of you."

After lunch, I spoke admiringly of what she had said, and I asked where she had found the courage. I was impressed with her reply. "Most days, I don't want to add to the noise. But today I noticed two other staff in that room who live in affordable housing and rely on food stamps. I could see them getting hurt. The others just forgot for a moment that they're not actually unkind people. I simply reminded them who they are."

Chameleons modify our style without compromising our message.

This woman normally retreats from controversy, but in this area, she chose to be bold—like a conversational chameleon—in order to serve others. The apostle Paul set an example of someone who yielded his personal communication-style preference to serve those he was sent to reach with the message of Jesus Christ. He describes this best in 1 Corinthians 9:19–23.

> For though I am free from all, I have made myself a servant to all, that I might win more of them. To the Jews I became as a Jew, in order to win Jews. To those under the law I became as one under the law (though not being myself under the law) that I might win those under the law. To those outside the law I

became as one outside the law (not being outside the law of God but under the law of Christ) that I might win those outside the law. To the weak I became weak, that I might win the weak. I have become all things to all people, that by all means I might save some. I do it all for the sake of the gospel, that I may share with them in its blessings.

No one would ever accuse Paul of being wishy-washy, and he clarifies in these verses the difference between style of message and content. According to the current situational need, chameleons modify our style without compromising our message. It takes thought and prayer, but it's possible and a worthwhile practice to cultivate.

Maybe you're a chameleon—sometimes hawk, other times turtle depending on the situation and audience. Chameleons vary our delivery, muting or magnifying ourselves depending on a variety of factors. We're shy about certain topics, bold about others or when properly motivated.

When you think about it, with such diverse conversational styles, it's a wonder any of us manage to communicate. Still, we have hope because we follow the one who is the Word. Identifying how we tend to approach hard conversations is the first step toward improving in the art of hard conversations.

ARTwork

Answer: What is the advantage of being a conversational chameleon? What's the most challenging aspect? How is it a benefit to the work of furthering the kingdom, and when might it detract from the work?

Read: Paul was a committed chameleon. Read 1 Corinthians 9:19–23 again. Then read Acts 17 to watch Paul in action engaging with three different communities.

Try: Embrace your design. Even when we repent of sin, we still don't look and act exactly alike. We can embrace God's unique idea of us. He designed each one with a personality, skills, strengths, and talents. He placed us in a time, culture, ethnicity, and family structure (Acts 17:26). When was the last time, rather than complaining about yourself to Him, you celebrated His idea of you as a form of praise? No time like now.

Lesson 5

A Nose Is Not an Eye

*If the foot should say, "Because I am not a hand, I
do not belong to the body," that would not make
it any less a part of the body. (1 Cor. 12:15)*

Interdependence is hardwired into God's design of the church. We resist it to our own loss.

My eyes glazed over as I struggled to pay attention as the financial chairperson talked about putting together a compensation package for our pastoral candidate. When he finished, he asked if we all had any questions.

"You lost me about five minutes in," I replied. "I'm sorry. I'm useless on this topic."

He laughed. "You look the way I felt back when we were creating the job description and you tried to explain inerrancy of Scripture."

Someone else piped up. "I love how we work together. Everyone has something different to offer. No one needs to be an expert on everything."

People are different. That should be a celebration, not a complaint. We appreciate variations on themes in nature, art, music, and other aspects of life. When it comes to communication, we forget we're free to revel in variety there too.

Our perspectives are so diverse, in fact, we even vary in what we would classify as hard conversations. A turtle may consider sharing his faith or debating a controversial or hard topic but be very comfortable conversing with the sick or comforting the dying. On the other hand, a hawk may thrive on defending the faith or confronting a false theology but balk at letting loved ones know how deeply they're valued. Chameleons rise and retreat as the situation demands. The kingdom benefits from this variety.

There's much to admire about hawks, turtles, and chameleons. God used Moses, Peter, and Paul. We need them all. Hawks keep the church talking and engaging with a boldness and certainty that inspires confidence. Turtles demonstrate necessary restraint and sensitivity, leading to an approachability that is valuable in outreach. Chameleons pay attention to cultural and situational differences that can inform the rest of us. Each style also has obvious drawbacks, but these drawbacks require us all to rely on Jesus.

While we encounter different hurdles, strategies for clearing them are something we can share. Spiritual maturity plays a role in this dynamic, but there are skills we can learn and steps we can take to improve everyone's experience discussing sensitive subjects.

It will never be easy, this side of glory. Hard conversations are likely to be hard, by their very definition, until we're home with God. But we can improve. We can all grow.

God knows who we are. He understands what we're made of. He embraces variety and appears to delight in working through us. More glory to Him, when He chooses the least likely among us to tackle the hardest topics.

Allow me to offer some assurance before we proceed.

> **The miracle of the church is that becoming more like Jesus doesn't make us identical but brings out the grain in our individual design.**

Remember that the ways of God, while often challenging, are also gracious and kind. God loves you and your personality. The miracle of the church is that becoming more like Jesus doesn't make us identical but brings out the grain in our individual design. He is patient with all our starts and stops. Be patient with yourself and others through these lessons.

And rest assured, the art of conversation is not all about the words. I've learned from paying attention to Jesus that the truth of Ecclesiastes 3:1 also applies to hard conversations. There's a time for everything. There's a time to speak and a time to remain silent. A time to utter words and a time to listen. A time to engage in dialogue and a time to instruct. A time to talk and a time to pray. A time to hear and a time to act.

Our faith isn't in words or conversations, but in the power of Christ. Words are just one vehicle for representing Him.

It's a mystery how God works through us—hawks, turtles, chameleons, and all the rest. Not a mystery to solve, but one to explore—together.

ARTwork

Answer: Think of times when you felt integral to or valued by the body of Christ. What contributed to this sense of belonging? How do you convey this to others?

Read: What does 1 Corinthians 12:12–31 say about why God chose to design the church with varied parts? What effect would there be if we all tried to be the same part?

Try: Start with a specific blessing. For some, hard conversations aren't the corrective ones, but the ones that feel too personal. And yet, if we make a habit of building up with our words, it lays a stronger foundation for the times we must confront. Before you start having hard conversations, exercise the habit of verbally blessing by encouraging others using specific observations.

"You're valued here at our church" is nice (and if that's what you've got, please go with that). But consider finding a personal comment, such as, "I've noticed how patient you are when managing your young children during the service." Or "You were kind to help Mr. Edwards to his seat." Or "It took courage to open up and tell our group what you've been facing."

The groundwork for hard conversations occurs more naturally when we've also used words to praise and encourage. When was the last time you verbally encouraged someone in your life who is different than you? How would your community be enriched if this was a common practice? Ask God to show you a way to offer a specific blessing to someone this week.

HEART OF THE ART PRACTICE

Read Exodus 3 and 4. Ask someone you trust to describe your conversational style. Listen. Don't interrupt or challenge any observations. Thank that person for honest feedback. What did you hear said?

UNIT 2

Fears, Arguments, and Invisible Walls

Lesson 1

Slamming into Walls

*They shall besiege you in all your towns, until your
high and fortified walls, in which you trusted, come
down throughout all your land. And they shall besiege
you in all your towns throughout all your land, which
the LORD your God has given you. (Deut. 28:52)*

We've all done it. Or, if not, we've seen someone do it. Turn around
to walk confidently through an opening, only to slam hard into a
screen or glass door we didn't initially see. It's funny in a comedy sketch.
Not so funny in conversations.

It's disorienting to think we're facing a doorway, only to discover a
wall, but it happens in discussions all the time. Most of us are aware
that the other person may put up a wall or guard against what we have
to say. So, we pray, use gentle words, and craft "I" messages such as
"I get worried when you don't call," rather than "You make me worry
when you're late." And yet, we still feel blocked.

What we're often unaware of is that *we've* erected a wall, invisible to
us. When we encounter this additional wall, it knocks the wind out of
us, and we wonder where we took a wrong turn. Internal walls may be

composed of fears, self-doubt, or pride. Other are devised of false perceptions, inflexibility, arguments, or misinformation.

Admittedly, some walls in relationships and conversations, just as in life, are useful. We call these "healthy boundaries." Later, we'll talk about times to stay silent, establishing conversational ground rules, and dealing with hurtful people. Right now, I want to consider pointless walls that only create barriers to fruitful conversations and deeper relationships.

I don't know a lot about physical walls, but my husband, Rob, is a carpenter. Years ago, we moved into his dream home (emphasis on *his*)—a rundown Victorian that required an overhaul. He deconstructed many interior walls—removing wallpaper, plaster, drywall, boards, metal, and sometimes framework. This was his way of understanding the project he'd undertaken (and God's way of developing a more Christlike character in me).

Rob says walls can be deceptive. Old walls may appear fragile and easy to demolish, when instead, they're a complex amalgam of materials that require backbreaking, painstaking work. Other walls seem hardy and strong but collapse with just a lean.

> **Soul renovation merits even more resources, research, and restorative attention than we invest in our impermanent, earthly homes.**

With the plethora of remodeling shows on television these days, most of us have some familiarity with relocating or modifying walls. Not every wall needs to be demolished but maybe just altered to allow for better airflow or visibility. Likewise, some of the internal walls we encounter may need to be dismantled or dismissed, while others only lowered (or descended) to communicate with others. We must agree that soul renovation merits even more resources, research, and restorative attention than we invest in our impermanent, earthly homes.

In 1 Corinthians 3:9–10, Paul encourages us to work alongside God in what He is building but also warns us to be careful how we build: "For we are God's fellow workers. You are God's field, God's building. According to the grace of God given to me, like a skilled master builder

I laid a foundation, and someone else is building upon it. Let each one take care how he builds upon it." We must test every spiritual material and every structure within our own internal framework to be sure it supports the integrity of a structure designed by the Master Builder.

ARTwork

Answer: In what ways can physical walls be necessary and helpful? In what ways can they be problematic?

Read: In Deuteronomy 28:52 God refers to the high and fortified walls in which the Israelites trusted. It's natural to erect walls of self-protection, but what does Psalm 18:2 say is the protection, the fortress, for those who follow God?

Try: Ask God to make you aware today every time you use words in self-defense or as self-protection. At day's end, prayerfully consider how those conversations could change if you exercise trust in God to be your fortress and protection.

Lesson 2

Turtle Walls

*For God gave us a spirit not of fear but of
power and love and self-control. (2 Tim. 1:7)*

Shelly's jaw dropped. "Aunt Iris, what are you doing at Bible study?"
Her aunt looked equally shocked. "I'm a Christian now. What are you doing here?"

"I'm a Christian too. How long have you been following Jesus? Why haven't you said anything?"

Her aunt wiped away tears. "Six years. I've longed to tell someone in the family, but I was afraid you'd all laugh or think I was judging you."

Shelly shook her head. "I've been afraid to speak up for the same reason. I became a believer three years ago. To think we were afraid when we could have been encouraging each other."

Shelly turned to me. "Our family complains about Christians all the time. Both of us have been staying quiet during those conversations. What if I had just spoken up once? Maybe my aunt and I would have discovered each other much earlier."

> **Our impulse is to retreat and hide, but God's imperative is to advance and redeem.**

If you're in turtle mode, you harbor a secret fear. I know, because I've harbored it too. This fear keeps us silent when we would speak. It holds us back from giving a more verbal witness of our faith, offering a firmer explanation of our beliefs about people's sinful behavior, or approaching a sensitive topic with loved ones.

The fear—which is clearly not from God since His Spirit is one of power, love, and self-control—stifles our voices, muzzles our testimonies, and leaves us feeling less than authentic during public (and often private) conversations. When touchy subjects arise, our impulse is to retreat and hide, but God's imperative is to advance and redeem.

We desperately want to overcome this fear for many reasons, but mostly because of love. Our love for God and others should free us, so we long to step into that freedom and help others do the same. It was imperative for Moses to overcome his fear of speaking out, not only so he could be free to obey God, but also because the freedom of his people, a people he loved, was at stake. Moses was transparent before God about his hesitations. He received the supports God provided (his miraculous staff and the companionship of Aaron), and he trusted God enough to act.

We know what the Bible teaches. We know Jesus cares that everyone hears the truth. Like Moses, we feel Him nudge us, prod us to weigh in, to represent Him, but we hesitate because of this secret fear.

When people speculate about our silence, they suppose we fear what people think of us. But that's not really it—well, not all of it. We love Jesus. We want to speak up on His behalf. We mostly want that more than we care what people think of us.

But what if rather than representing Jesus, we bungle the whole thing?

What if we embarrass other Christians with our lame phrases or an inadequate defense of our faith? What if our inept words create dissension within the body of Christ or cause serious hurt to another believer? What if we drive our loved one away? What if we just plain get our facts wrong and make statements we can't back up, confirming that person's thinking that Christians don't know what they're talking about?

Like the wall in Jericho (Josh. 6), our what-ifs pile on, one atop the other, until we're trapped on the other side of our intentions, feeling small and silent. It's that wall of what-ifs that looms between us and stepping into conversational freedom. It becomes a kind of stronghold.

> **Our secret fear is that we will bumble conversations and blemish God's greatness rather than confirm it.**

Our secret fear is that we will bumble conversations and blemish God's greatness rather than confirm it. If our fumbled words make others feel unacceptable to us, and then they feel unacceptable to God, we would loathe that.

Shelly and her aunt prayed for their loved ones. They were concerned about being mocked, but mostly because they weren't confident they'd be able to articulate their answers. They sat silently enclosed in their own what-if walls, but if one of them had embraced the "spirit . . . of power and love and self-control" by speaking up, they would have discovered they weren't alone.

We understand how pivotal these conversations are. We've heard people say just one bad comment from a Christian turned them off to Jesus. Or one uncomfortable confrontation with a fellow Christian crippled them in their walk with Christ. How terrifying!

Like those bad dreams when we try to scream but no sounds come out, our awareness of the stakes tethers us to our silence. Who are we to speak for Jesus? Who are we to confront someone? Better to hang back long enough for the conversation to take a turn. Let our lives do the talking. That's what matters anyway, isn't it?

So, we console ourselves knowing there are plenty of other people addressing these hard subjects. Smart people. People with gifts. God's thinkers. Conversational hawks. Stammering Moses is our poster child. Smooth-tongued Aarons abound. Maybe we're off the hook.

But Jesus persists in nudging us from our shells. He persists because there are always conversations happening when none of these articulate Christians is around. Even if they were, they don't know this person sitting across from us or posting to our wall. Not like we do.

They can't engage with the person asking us the hard questions or wrestling with a sin issue or a serious life challenge. They aren't the one seeing this person's face, aware of the confusion, anger, or angst. We not only know this person's crisis, but we also know the backstory. Our understanding might provide the perfect framework for a unique response, if we only dared speak.

Even in turtle mode, we love God and others just enough to be uncomfortable sitting in silence when it's time the truth should be spoken. We sense that if we loved Him and them just a little bit more, if we had just a bit more skill with words, if we had a modicum of direction and coaching, these conditions would free us to join the conversation. After all, the Jericho wall fell.

ARTwork

Answer: Think about the last conversation you heard when you felt that you should speak up but didn't. What concerns, thoughts, or fears created your what-if wall?

Read: Conversational walls may be invisible to us, but is anything hidden from God? What does Psalm 33:13–22 say about relying on human means for protection as opposed to relying on God?

Try: Practice transparency. When we stop worrying about defending ourselves or presenting a certain appearance, it opens a door for us to be genuine and transparent, which is often more powerful than eloquence. We can admit to another person that we don't know what to say but want to express our support. It may sound something like this: "I never know what to say in situations like this. I'm afraid of saying the wrong thing, but you're important to me. I want to be in this with you in any way I can—praying, talking, listening, providing practical help—whatever you need. How can I show you the love both God and I have for you?"

Practice this. You may find it useful when you least expect it.

Lesson 3

Hawk Walls

But when Simon Peter saw it, he fell down at
Jesus' knees, saying, "Depart from me, for
I am a sinful man, O Lord." (Luke 5:8)

I've followed Jesus since I was a child, but there's one zealous evangelist in a Rhode Island airport who just wouldn't be convinced. My children and I were waiting for their dad to return from a business trip when the twenty-something woman beside us asked if I was interested in spiritual things.

"Deeply," I replied.

Her eyes widened with excitement. "If you have a minute, I'd love to talk with you about Jesus."

"That would be wonderful. I'm a Christian too."

She frowned. "Well, just going to church doesn't make you a Christian."

I switched my baby to the other hip. "I'm aware of that. I truly do know and love Jesus."

"Some people *think* they know Jesus, but really they're just following a religion."

I nodded warily. "Sure, but that's not me. I know Jesus died for me and rose again. I study the Bible. I teach my children about Jesus."

She cocked her head as one would at a very feeble person. "It's okay that you don't understand. I have good news. Jesus loves you anyway. If you'll just let me explain, I can lead you into a relationship that will ensure you eternal life."

I lowered my voice, reminding myself to be kind. "But I already have eternal life."

"No, no, I'm sorry. You don't. But you can, if you just let me explain how."

"You're new to evangelism, aren't you, honey?"

"It's normal to feel some anger when you come under the conviction of the Holy Spirit. Jesus can help you."

"Oh, believe me, Jesus is helping me right now." Restraining me from unleashing a lecture on this determined sister who would not be deterred from saving my already-saved soul. As I quietly judged her, though, Jesus reviewed with me the flip book of my early days sharing the gospel, and I backed off. (Sigh.) Log-removal process engaged—again.

Hawks can be tempted to focus more on our plan than on the person before us.

Like Peter, we hawks are full of love for Jesus but too often, we race ahead thinking we know best how to accomplish what He wants. In Luke 5:1–11, Jesus showed Peter that not only did Jesus know His business better than Peter, but He even knew Peter's business better than Peter. We can be sure that lesson served Peter well in the years to come in fostering necessary humility and reliance on God in all things, a worthwhile lesson for hawks.

In hawk mode, we're not afraid of anything. Okay, that's not the whole truth, but we aren't afraid of conflict or of making people uncomfortable. We boldly speak what no one spoke before.

Like turtles, we love Jesus and we know the truth, but we speak it easily, without apology. We wish turtles would start carrying their fair share of the heavy conversational lifting. Turtles wish we would take a breath.

We feel we're neglecting our calling if we aren't stirring the pot. If too many people agree with us, we worry that we've wandered off track. We represent Jesus, and our greatest fear is falling down on the job. We're not about to be put off by something as fickle as other people's feelings or fellow Christians' sensitivities. There's just too much at risk and too few people speaking up.

Still, we're aware that sometimes we've caused needless hurt. We know that, like the eager evangelist in the airport, we're prone to shift into autopilot and steamroll our listeners. That bothers us, but we argue that it seems like the unavoidable by-product of making people aware they're in danger of missing or misrepresenting Jesus.

We wouldn't be delicate about warning others of an oncoming train or the edge of a cliff. These are dangerous times, so out of our love for others and obedience to Christ, we boldly sound the alarm. Better to be bold than to balk. That's our motto, and it's not all bad.

Still, others encourage us to invest more time listening. While we see the wisdom of this, we worry it's a road to diluting the message. If only we could envision a clear path to engage in listening that would facilitate effective truth-telling.

God calls us all, even His beloved hawks, to slow down and listen (James 1:19). The last thing we want to do is resist Him, but we've developed this habit of talking that's hard to break. Like my would-be evangelist, hawks can be tempted to focus more on our plan than on the person before us.

Plus, hawks have our own what-if wall, only our wall is more of a perch. Where turtles' walls are mostly devised of fears, in hawk mode we use arguments and explanations as building material.

Hawks can become so far removed from others, we only hear our own voices.

It may be that these sound reasonings helped us see the truth, so we know they are useful. While we initially scale each what-if to get closer to God, unfortunately, hawks can become so far removed from others, we only hear our own voices. Hawks sometimes forget the pathway we took to reach the place where we now stand and wonder why others won't just leap to where we are.

Jesus didn't reside on some unreachable height. His feet touched the dusty earth as He broke bread with both rulers and renegades. He came to us. Yes, He came preaching, but He also met us where we were and heard our cries. Listening lessens the distance between us and those Jesus loves. But listening requires faith.

We believe listening is important, in theory, but we're a little suspect of it in practice. What if we listen to others, but they take our listening as approval of their wrongdoing? What if we slow our speech, but others see it as compromising or diluting the truth?

What if softening our words leads to a softening of obedience? What if everyone starts listening, and no one is speaking the hard truth? Won't that lead to more people lost and separated from Jesus?

If that eager evangelist had listened to me, we might have had a rich spiritual conversation. Instead, I was left wondering if she was a sister in Christ or a member of a pseudo-Christian cult.

What if we could slow down and listen so well that when we did speak, our words had a better context for moving our listeners? What if, like ground personnel waving flashlights on the tarmac, our ears could guide our words to a secure landing on the runway of a person's mind?

After all, we want our words to open hearts, not erect more walls.

Even in hawk mode, we love God and others just enough to be uncomfortable talking over everyone, when we might speak more effective words if we listened first.

ARTwork

Answer: Think about the last time you knew you were talking too much—going on without letting others speak, interrupting, or lecturing. What were the signs warning you to pause? Why did you ignore them?

Read: Read Psalm 116 and then Genesis 16:7–14. In the case of the psalmist and of Hagar, what was their response to being heard by God? What does this tell us about the inherent power of listening?

Try: Seek clarification. Both the psalmist and Hagar felt heard by God partly because they received something from Him. We sometimes hesitate to listen because we don't want to "give in" to others, but often we don't have a clear understanding of what they want (and neither do they). Asking for clarification before we respond to someone can help both parties. We may be able to offer more than we realized. For example, the conversation may sound like the following:

Coworker: I feel as though you don't support me.

Clarifying question: What would it look like if I was supporting you in the way you need?

Or it might sound like the following example:

Congregant: I wish you were preaching more from the Word.

Pastor: Well, that's my goal too. Let's consider my last two sermons. What would be different about them if I was preaching more from the Word?

Lesson 4

Chameleon Walls

I, Paul, myself entreat you, by the meekness
and gentleness of Christ—I who am humble
when face to face with you, but bold toward
you when I am away! (2 Cor. 10:1)

You may be, like I am, a chameleon.

In personal situations, I can come across as reserved. For years I struggled with advocating for myself or asking for anything that might put others out. If I was served something in a restaurant that I didn't order, I would rather eat it than complain and send it back. When visiting people, I would go out of my way to need nothing, which is completely unrealistic and usually more of a concern for a kind host than a help.

Friends who knew me in my twenties chided me often for not speaking up, until one Sunday, I was asked to report on a Christian missions conference I'd attended. The church had underwritten the cost of my travel, so I was eager to say thank you. More than that, I'd returned with a new fire for advancing the kingdom of God, and I shared that fire during my ten-minute presentation.

Afterward, friends surrounded me with expressions of shock and delight. One remarked, "Who are you and where have you been hiding? We don't know this Lori, but we'd like to know her more."

This confused me because I felt they were accusing me of being false or appearing to be two different people. It took time to understand the work God was doing in me to transform a girl who was more naturally a turtle to speak up in positions where a hawk-like nature was more needed. Now, I am more comfortable giving Him credit for helping me respond to each situation with the approach that is called for, even when that means transcending my natural inclinations.

Chameleons crave camouflage but can conquer when called out by Christ.

By default, chameleons cling to comfort. We're passionate about representing Jesus, but we struggle to complain about incorrect food orders, never mind standing up for unpopular biblical truths. We dislike causing discomfort. We know and love Jesus, but in the company of others, frankly He makes us nervous. Chameleons crave camouflage but can conquer when called out by Christ.

On the other hand, we're students of God's Word and take it seriously. At times our passion for Jesus and biblical truth has led us to stalk others like unwitting prey, unleashing windy word gusts that blew them away, instead of drawing them into the family of God and right living.

I've had much to learn and am still learning the art of hard conversations. Despite my nature and my what-if walls, I've become adept at engaging others in tough talks. Honestly, though, my inner turtle still prays someone else will speak up so I don't have to. Every. Single. Time. And my hawk nature rambles on without listening, far too often.

Despite the fact that my walls are patchy from the varying materials, I continue to smack into them. What if I remain quiet, but miss this opportunity? What if I speak up, but my nerves take over and I say the wrong things? What if I'm not obeying the Holy Spirit? What if I'm trying to play the Holy Spirit in this person's life? Chameleons try to blend into the scenery, so no one suspects this raging internal debate between our fears and arguments.

We're all students in this ongoing work and none of us masters, but there is one who is Master of all. So we hold out hope for growth and effective change—in the meekest turtle, the boldest hawk, and the twitchiest chameleon.

ARTwork

Answer: What situations or people bring out your turtle tendency and when are you most likely to engage your hawk style? Is the switch more likely to be influenced by subject, situation, or the individuals present?

Read: In 2 Corinthians 10, Paul explains to the church of Corinth why at times he is bold and at other times appears meek. Where does Paul seat his confidence and how can this inform your own?

Try: Observe. Paul paid attention wherever he traveled, to the people, their culture, and their values. He did this to better serve them and understand what illustrations would be effective when sharing the gospel. Ask yourself what you can learn about the people in your life through observing—their possessions, clothing, entertainments, habits, and interests. Ask God how these observations can inform your approach to conversations. An individual's culture, interests, profession, and hobbies can provide reference points for initiating conversations or for elucidating biblical truths.

Lesson 5

Detecting Invisible Walls

Search me, O God, and know my heart!
Try me and know my thoughts!
And see if there be any grievous way in me,
and lead me in the way everlasting!
(Ps. 139:23–24)

While these walls are invisible to us, they're neither undetectable nor insurmountable, not with Jesus. Before we explore how to either dismantle, dismiss, or descend them, though, allow me to tell a story that illustrates how to detect them.

Once, I supervised a young man who was skilled in his job, but continually rubbed clients the wrong way. One of our workplace values was relationship building. While clients acknowledged Darren knew what he was talking about, they avoided him unless they needed information.

My inner turtle hoped he'd spontaneously develop people skills through one of our group trainings or by osmosis, so I procrastinated correcting him. Didn't happen. Soon, I knew, my supervisor would confront me if I didn't deal with it.

I scheduled a meeting with Darren, so I would have a deadline. Then, I invited God into a hard conversation with me. "What," I prayed, "created the wall causing me to delay what should be a straightforward conversation?" After I prayed, I listed my fears about the conversation and my arguments for delaying it.

There's more to this story that we'll cover in the next unit, but for now, it's important to understand the value of prayerful reflection prior to initiating hard conversations. Or, if we're midconflict or hard times and anticipate pop-up conversations that promise tension, we're wise to practice this reflection with regularity.

This isn't something that needs to be overthought. It's simply about pulling away from the situation to spend time alone with God and asking God to reveal what barriers you may be putting up that you can't see. James outlines the process in James 4:6–10. Essentially, he instructs us to submit to God, resist the devil, and draw near to God. We're encouraged to be purified and to humble ourselves. It's this attitude of humility and submission to Him that pleases God.

God's Word tells us humility is the pathway to God's presence and grace.

This practice served me well another time when I was in a small group Bible study and found myself anxious and irritated as one gentleman shared his responses to the week's questions. The thoughts I was having were neither supportive nor generous toward this brother in Christ and I worried what would happen if anyone asked my thoughts. So I quietly prayed, "Lord, why am I so bothered by him and what do I do?"

Suddenly, I realized what I was feeling was conflicted. This gentleman had hurt another person in the group and they were still working this out. I was torn between my loyalty to the injured person and my desire to support growth in this man. It's normal to feel conflicted. We're only human and it is challenging to sort through the dynamics of church relationships. This brief prayer and reflection eased my anxiety. I reminded myself that God doesn't expect me to have every answer or resolve everyone else's problem. Reducing my irritation made room for compassion and grace.

Anger, pride, and self-righteousness are powerful emotions. They deceive us into imagining they're great defenses against attack when they're just barriers to growth and change. We can work blind from behind our barricades or improve our views and emerge to risk success. God's Word tells us humility is the pathway to God's presence and grace.

▌Better defended by God than by our own devices.

The beauty of becoming aware of invisible walls is that our own walls (once we acknowledge them) are completely within our power to destroy. They're frequently barriers our well-intentioned, faulted selves erected to defend us against possible attack, so we address them by dismantling, descending, or dismissing our own defenses. Better defended by God than by our own devices.

God's Word and prayer are powerful avenues for informing our perspective. Reflecting on relevant Scripture, or bouncing our thoughts off another mature, trusted believer, can illuminate our what-if wall.

ARTwork

Answer: Remember a hard conversation where you were nervous at the start, but by the end, you felt relieved. How can that experience help you prepare for another hard conversation?

Read: In Jonah 1–3, Jonah goes to great lengths to avoid having a hard conversation with the Ninevites. What wall did Jonah anticipate? What was the actual barrier to the Ninevites receiving God's message?

Try: Reflect on a hard conversation you've had recently or anticipate having. Get alone with your Bible and a notebook. Read James 4:1–12 and ask God to illuminate any barriers or "invisible walls" within you that inhibit growth or change in that relationship. How could the next conversation be different?

HEART OF THE ART PRACTICE

Listening Hawk Style

Change happens best in stages. If your style is to speak boldly, learn to use bold statements that encourage others to speak. Commanding statements sound assertive while acting like open-ended questions. Sentences like "Tell me more about that," "I'm interested in hearing why you feel that way," "Help me understand that idea," or "There's a story behind that thought that I'd love to hear," are bold, but lead to conversation.

Or ask others to quantify where they stand and tell you why. For example, "On a scale of one to ten, how invested are you in resolving this conflict?" When they choose a number, ask them why it's that number and not a lesser number. Ask them what would move them from the number they chose to the next highest. This is a hawk-like way of eliciting information and providing opportunity to listen. Hawks love using these types of sentences because they express zeal and passion, while still tossing the conversation to the other participant.

Creation Contemplation for Turtles

One way to fortify confidence in God's desire to use even those of us who tend to be turtles is to pay attention to creation. God placed power in hurricanes and gale force winds, but He also infused power in dandelions that grow up through cement and infants who arrest hardened old men with just a smile.

Imagine that as God goes about the work of furthering His kingdom, He knows His tools better than anyone. He knows which situations call for a hammer and which might require a fine chisel. When you're called into action, place yourself in His hands, and trust He knows what He's about. When you're wondering if He can use you, look for an example of your style in creation and meditate on it.

UNIT 3

Addressing Our Walls

Lesson 1

The Ministry of Wall Removal

*For he himself is our peace, who has made us
both one and has broken down in his flesh
the dividing wall of hostility. (Eph. 2:14)*

Detecting walls is our first step, but we can't stop there if our goal is to reach another person with our words. Spiritual, emotional, and mental walls are as real as physical walls, and when they are present, they are just as significant a barrier to forward progress.

First, let's acknowledge that it is possible to communicate through walls. We do it all the time. What's possible, however, is not always what's preferable. My husband and children used to reach me through walls.

"Honey, have you seen my keys?"

"Mom, can I go over to Joel's house?"

"Mom, where are you? I don't know what to wear."

Inevitably, I'd be on the phone. Excusing myself and covering the phone, I'd try to quell the questions. "I'm on the phone." This only led to misunderstanding.

"What? I didn't lose my phone, I lost my keys."

"What? Why do I have to stay home? That's not fair."

"Mom, I can't figure it out alone. I need you."

52

Finally, in frustration, I'd end my call and holler back, "If you want to talk with me, get up and make the effort to come where I am!"

Rather than find me when they needed something, my family hollered from where they were. It was an inefficient (lazy) method of communication and usually an exercise in aggravation, this shouting through walls. However, it happens in conversation all the time. People do manage, with considerable exertion, to communicate through their walls, but how much easier (and with fewer misunderstandings) would it be to remove the barriers?

> **Shouting, frustration, and miscommunication are sure signs of walls that would be best addressed.**

Shouting, frustration, and miscommunication are sure signs of walls that would be best addressed. We can talk through walls, but working to get past the walls demonstrates our commitment to both the person and the conversation. God could have found other ways to reach us, but He chose to break down every wall by becoming one of us. He is the example we follow; should we do any less in our efforts to love our families, churches, and communities?

Working on clear communication is daunting, I know, but consider the turmoil and energy required to fix miscommunications or to constantly repeat ourselves through walls. Effort in relationships is inevitable. Most of us would rather labor effectively, though, than find we've worked hard for no result.

Sometimes walls were erected for what started out as good reasons. In Joshua 6, we read the story of Jericho. The walls of that city were built for protection for the people. When the Israelites entered the land, the leaders of the city locked themselves in tight against them. The problem was, these walls kept the people of God out and God wanted them in.

This fortress appeared impossible to destroy to Joshua and his people, but God told them to march around the walls and watch Him work. In our times, marching around Jericho is more of an inside job. We have barriers within us that will make reaching out and truly ministering to others a greater challenge. They seem just as impossible to destroy as

Jericho did to the Israelites, but God hasn't changed. And if we dismantle, dismiss, or descend our walls, the people we're hoping to reach will be more likely to reconsider their need for theirs.

We worry about the work of walls, while God wonders why we won't just start walking around them and watch Him act. The sooner we invite Him into the equation, the sooner we'll taste the fruits of all our labors.

ARTWORK

Answer: When has miscommunication been a problem in one of your relationships? What made it frustrating? What changed to make it less so?

Read: Read the story of Joshua at Jericho in Joshua 6. Consider how Joshua might have responded to God's command if he doubted God's ability or refused to walk in faith.

Try: Put conversation in motion. You may find, as I have, that many successful hard conversations occur during an activity. Insistence on sitting across from each other maintaining steady eye contact while chatting may only increase discomfort. Instead, schedule a conversation while playing a game of one-on-one basketball, painting a wall, stitching a quilt, walking babies in strollers, or exercising. Activity can provide a healthy outlet for tension, ready object lessons, or a sense of cooperation even when what's being discussed is personal or potentially contentious.

Lesson 2

Dismantling

But the LORD said to Samuel, "Do not look on his appearance or on the height of his stature, because I have rejected him. For the LORD sees not as man sees: man looks on the outward appearance, but the LORD looks on the heart." (1 Sam. 16:7)

Dismantling is largely turtle work.

Let's revisit the situation I had with Darren. My major what-if was,

"What if Darren resists my assessment of his job skills?" This fear was the primary barrier between me and this conversation. I know that God repeatedly calls us to courage, not to fear, so first, I reminded myself of two Scriptures on this call. Second Timothy 1:7 says, "For God gave us a spirit not of fear but of power and love and self-control." Psalm 118:6 reads, "The LORD is on my side; I will not fear. What can man do to me?"

After reading these, I challenged myself with a counter what-if: "What if Darren does know he's not good at building relationships but has no idea how to change?" This new what-if acted like a wrecking ball on my wall, and soon more what-ifs (ones that encouraged me to be excited about the conversation) fluttered about with the debris from my wall.

What if he was aware of the problem and was either open to solutions or understood my concerns because they mirrored his own? What if my delay was increasing his anxiety about his performance when I could teach him skills to improve?

What if I spent less time fearing failure and more time preparing to see God work?

What if I spent less time fearing failure and more time preparing to see God work?

I rapidly became barrier-free on my end. My wall was down. Deciding to open our conversation with a question gave me confidence to remain calm and led to the following exchange.

"Hi, Darren. I want us to discuss how you're doing in this position. You bring some great strengths to your work and like all of us, have areas that could use bolstering. The two keys to being good at our work here are (a) knowing what we're talking about regarding our subject, and (b) being able to engage with clients and build strong relationships. What do you see as your strength, or needs around these two skills?"

He thought about it for only a moment. "I definitely know what I'm talking about. Even other staff come to me for advice. But I've never been good at building relationships with people. I heard that in my last job. I don't know how to fix that."

"We value your expertise in our subject area. You're right about that being your strength. Are you interested in learning ways to improve at relationship building? As you know, it's a nonnegotiable skill for this position."

"To be honest, I've started looking for another job. I'll try if you think it will help, but I'm not sure how much I can change."

We implemented training, but within the month, Darren gave his notice. We both felt good about his decision. He found work more suited to his skills, and I was prepared for his departure. He even thanked me for our conversation.

Prayerful reflection and God's Word had helped open my eyes to the wall I'd erected. Using an open-ended question to start our conversation assisted me in learning if Darren had any walls of his own. I wish he'd been willing to learn new skills, but at least there was more integrity in our parting than there would have been without the conversation. He gained a better understanding of how he works best, and I gained a model to use for future conversations.

This would have happened quicker if I'd demolished my what-if wall faster. I had imagined that he'd put up a wall when really it was my wall that delayed our chat, and dismantling it was the solution to our shared problem.

We're most likely to become trapped behind a conversational wall in turtle mode. Many of us turtles benefit from investing time in prayerful reflection (as I did before meeting with Darren) about what comprises our own barriers to conversation and then some wall dismantling.

Here's what that can look like.

Rather than question God's ways (God, why ask me to do this?), it makes more sense to question our hesitations. *Why am I reluctant to speak up?* List the reasons you believe the conversation should happen and then list every reason you're procrastinating (your what-ifs).

Next, consider Scriptures that speak to your hesitation, as well as God's character, and then apply those to your what-if wall. For example, is fear ever a reason not to do anything? If God calls us to do a thing, will He not equip us for it? Is it most loving to the other person to have the conversation or to avoid it? We utilize biblically informed arguments to weaken our walls one what-if at a time. (If you're unfamiliar with God's Word, ask assistance of someone more biblically knowledgeable on this.)

Finally, we blast our wall by countering the weakened what-ifs that talk us out of speaking with what-ifs that move us toward the conversation. What if God has chosen this conversation to start a transforming work, and we're privileged to witness His power in action? What if this conversation is the last key conversation in a long line of others God has inspired people to have with this person? What if we've been wrong about this person and by not speaking up, we keep ourselves locked inside deceptive ideas?

The hardest part of Jericho was deciding to start the march.

Jericho looked like impossible work, but God felled the wall with minimum effort on the part of His people. I imagine the hardest part of Jericho was deciding to start the march. This can be true for many of the walls blocking effective and fruitful conversations.

I once led a Bible study for women who had no previous experience with the Bible. As we arrived for the first meeting, each indicated surprise that one of the expected participants had agreed to attend. Their comments were variations on a theme.

"Oh, don't get your hopes up about Gloria getting into the Bible."

Head shaking and tongue clicking. "She's a wild one, Gloria. She certainly has never considered living according to anything that's in the Bible."

One woman ticked off Gloria's sins with her fingers. "She's living with her newest boyfriend—and she's had *a lot* of boyfriends. She was Jewish but doesn't believe in anything now, except what's trendy. Plus, she's one of those feminists. If she comes, she'll attack you over every little thing. But don't worry; she won't show."

Initially, their cautions ratcheted the usual anxiety I have whenever beginning a new Bible study. I scanned the material I planned to cover and mentally prepared defenses for anything I could anticipate she might find offensive. In other words, the walls these women had built inspired me to erect my own.

Then I looked around the table. Not one of these women had ever spent time in God's Word. I knew they all faced their share of trouble and had rarely considered God's commands when making major decisions. I had hope for each of them. Why wouldn't I be hopeful for Gloria? It may even be an advantage that her "sins" arrived ahead of her. I had no doubt there were some trailing behind those already arrived. God rapidly helped me reduce my wall to rubble and be open to whatever He was about to do.

Gloria not only came to the study, but she also attended faithfully, raised thoughtful questions, took immediately to Jesus, and applied every passage as soon as she learned it. The woman "most likely to cause a problem" transformed into the woman most in love with Jesus and most likely to tell her friends.

It was an important lesson to me that (a) what-if walls are contagious, so there's value in declining to adopt another's perspective without filtering it through biblical truth, and (b) walls come down faster than they go up if we're open to identifying and addressing them.

We never know when God's armies are on their seventh march around the wall of someone's soul. It's best we prepare to watch walls fall, as readily as we prepare for them to remain in place.

ARTwork

Answer: Describe a time when you were caught off guard by someone's interest in a spiritual topic. What had been your initial impression of that person? How might you have approached that person differently if you'd known how ready he or she was to talk?

Read: Read 1 Samuel 16:7 and then turn to John 4:1–30. What do you imagine people saw when they viewed the woman at the well? Why do you suppose we rely on our own understanding and sight, more than on the unseen work of God?

Try: Counter what-ifs. Consider a hard conversation you've delayed. List the what-ifs that comprise your wall. Now, identify several counter what-ifs that could be just as possible as the ones fueling your delay.

Lesson 3

Descending

For I have come down from heaven, not to do my
own will but the will of him who sent me. (John 6:38)

Now, if dismantling what-if walls is turtle work, descending them is work cut out for hawks. Hawks tend to ascend the walls we build. The valuable arguments that helped cement our convictions and increase our courage sometimes become perches from which we look down on others.

We are very aware of our wall, and part of us believes we can do all God calls us to do from a great height. It's anxiety-provoking to consider spending more time "below" than is necessary to swoop in on our listeners.

We worry we won't find our way back up and fret that time spent there will lead to no good. The ascent required so much effort, we can't imagine the answer to reaching others is to descend. We try shouting instructions or simply modeling our faith from above. We certainly don't want to dismantle truths that built our convictions, but neither do we want them to be barriers to reaching others. Often, it's the first step that presents the greatest challenge.

I remember the first (and last) time I rappelled off a cliff. I was in my twenties and single, so I volunteered to assist a young man from church by chaperoning a teen mountain-climbing trip. So focused was I on gaining this man's attention, I ignored the fact that I had no experience rappelling. It didn't take long for me to garner his attention, but it wasn't the kind that earned me favor.

Tapping into my hawk nature, I volunteered to be first down the cliff. The harness and belay made it appear safe—that is, until it was time for that initial step. My brain instructed my legs to push off, but they refused to comply. They were busy processing the panic message my eyes relayed when I made the mistake of looking down.

The teens offered encouragement—at first. Then came pointed

instructions, accompanied by impatient sighs. Finally, I heard muttered conspiracies to give me a firm push. After an embarrassingly long hesitation, I leaped. Once I started down the cliff face, I shook my head. Why had I waited so long?

> **We need to come alongside people, not tower over them, to make effective connections.**

I could have chaperoned just as easily from the top. But stepping off bridged a lot of distance between me and those teens. They accepted me even though they'd seen me hesitant and afraid. Okay, probably *because* they saw me hesitant and afraid, but it helped that I was willing to join them in the descent. From then on, every time I taught about facing a fear, they remembered watching me face one. We need to come alongside people, not tower over them, to make effective connections.

Some of us may understand this quickly. Swooping off our perch is fine if we remain grounded and don't just swoop back. Others may need to make the painful descent one handhold at a time. No matter what method we choose, it's preferable to looking down on those we're attempting to engage in conversation. It's disheartening to hear someone shout from above but uplifting to receive encouragement from someone who comes alongside.

It helps us hawks to remember that Jesus "came down," as He told the Jews in John 6:38: "For I have come down from heaven, not to do my own will but the will of him who sent me."

We want to be like Jesus. He descended from the heights without compromising His character, testimony, or obedience. Strong encouragement, that. Descending our walls isn't about compromise. It's about optimal positioning.

When I was learning karate at age forty, I was terrible at it. To say I'm not a natural athlete is quite an understatement. The instructors were clearly frustrated that what others seemed to understand quickly had to be broken down for me.

One sensei (teacher) was more patient than the others. He too had struggled with the moves initially. He remembered how he'd broken them down in order to learn them, and he dissected them for me. He asked how I learn best and incorporated that understanding into his approach with me. I was eventually able to earn my black belt because he "came down" from the height of his third degree and invested his time in my instruction.

What can this look like for us in hard conversations?

First, ask God to continually remind you of the path you took to understand Him and the truths you're trying to convey. Cultivate humility at every opportunity.

Second, study passages like Mark 2. Jesus didn't need to ask people questions to gain information, but He did ask them questions. His questions were designed to incite them to engage their minds just before He imparted truth. Let this and passages like it instruct and inspire you.

Finally, start where they already are. Prepare questions, taking into consideration what the person may already be feeling or asking.

For example, if you're trying to inspire someone to attend a Bible study on a regular basis, you may start by asking, "Have you ever been confused when something you heard on television seemed to contradict what we teach at church? What have you tried to resolve that confusion?" Or, if you'd like to have a conversation about salvation, you might say, "We've known each other a long time, and you know I have a relationship with Jesus. Was there ever a time when you considered following Him? If you don't mind me asking, what led you to choose not to make that commitment?"

We become more like Jesus when we descend from our walls to reach others. After all, He became one of us to initiate the ultimate hard conversation in a voice we could hear.

ARTWORK

Answer: Has anyone come alongside you in a way that made a lasting impact? What factors about that experience made you feel supported and not judged?

Read: Elijah was a great prophet. In 2 Kings 2, he's ready to depart this world. Elisha had walked beside Elijah. As they parted, Elisha requested a double portion of the spirit he witnessed in Elijah's life. What would you want people to see in your life that they desire to imitate?

Try: Reflect. A simple tip for all styles is to use a technique called reflection. Before we respond in conversation, repeat what the other person said as in "So, your husband is gone all the time and you feel overwhelmed." Or "Wow, you are really feeling stressed right now." Or "You're saying something has moved you to consider following Jesus. Tell me more about that." This slows down the hawks and gives the turtles time to gather thoughts.

Lesson 4

Dismissing

*Jesus answered them, "I also will ask you
one question, and if you tell me the answer,
then I also will tell you by what authority
I do these things." (Matt. 21:24)*

Countless conversations arise when we won't have time or opportunity for the kind of reflection we've discussed so far. There is a kind of wrecking ball method, however, that we all can employ to make quick work of (effectively dismissing) our pop-up walls. Jesus used this method to great effect, and so can we. It's called the "single question strategy." Let me illustrate it, then explain.

As I set my tray on the lunch table, it was evident from the tense faces that my friends were in a heated discussion. It seemed to center around Lydia, an intelligent and well-spoken woman. Ted, studying for the ministry, leaned toward her, red-faced.

"How can you even think we'll entertain this idea? God isn't female. There's no way it's okay to refer to Him as She," Ted said.

Lydia was near tears. "I didn't imagine you'd understand, but lots of other people do. Isn't God Spirit? Aren't the women at the table made in Her image?"

Another student, Maria, made a face. "Urgh! I'm a woman and I can't imagine changing God's pronouns. Doesn't He present Himself to us as a Father?"

Lydia's hands clenched, and she rocked from side to side, trying to explain. "No. I need this, and I need you all to accept me on this. Gender-inclusive language in the church must include God. I just can't pray to a male God. I won't."

Ted noticed I'd finished saying grace (having made it last as long as possible) and invited me into the debate. "Lori, you don't support referring to God as a She, do you?"

I inhaled and looked at Lydia, who seemed moments from crumbling. "I wasn't here at the start of the discussion. Has anyone asked you, Lydia, why this subject is important to you?"

Lydia shook her head. She then explained that she'd been in counseling for abuse she'd suffered at the hands of her father and brother. She was learning to acknowledge and cope with her anger against men. This need to refer to God as She sprang from deep wounds and pain.

As she spoke, the heat left our conversation. We didn't change our minds about the subject, but the nature of the exchange became one of love toward Lydia and brainstorming ways we could all support her healing.

A single question can help us get our bearings and blast barrier walls.

When a hard conversation springs up, a single question can help us get our bearings and blast barrier walls. One question can determine if a person is sincerely seeking or hoping to agitate. This was a favorite strategy of Jesus (Matt. 15:1–9; 17:24–27). He often disarmed the religious rulers or an angry mob with a single question. One piece of follow-up information can serve us in dismissing pop-up shield walls that arise reflexively and transforming our response into one with greater effect.

For example, when a coworker asks our position on abortion, it helps to first ask, "Why do you ask?" It could be the question is very personal for her. If that were the case, it would be valuable to ask a few more questions, including, "Is this a subject you're wrestling with right now?" Maybe she or her daughter is pregnant with an unwanted baby. It shouldn't change your position on abortion, but it does merit a longer, more intimate conversation about God's compassion and local resources.

Or it could turn out the person is an agitator looking to stir up trouble for us in our workplace. If that's the case, we're perfectly in our right to ask a follow-up question: "Are you truly interested in what I believe is the biblical teaching around abortion, or are you just asking to find out 'what side' I'm on?"

If the person is truly interested, that's a conversation. If that person is just looking for sides, feel free to disengage with "I only have a conversation of this importance with people truly seeking answers, not with people just looking for an argument."

Or "I base my opinions on my faith in Jesus and biblical teaching." Or "Topics of life and death are holy for me, not something I engage in casually. If you want to have a serious conversation, let's schedule a time. Otherwise, I'd be happy to choose a more work-related topic."

This isn't a delay tactic for turtles, nor is it a control tactic for hawks (although it could be seen this way). Asking a question before answering helps us tease out others' actual needs and serves as a reminder that we have no obligation to operate on the world's agenda. We answer to Jesus and, like Him, we're here to follow our Father's agenda, no one else's.

ARTwork

Answer: Have you ever felt trapped into a conversation about a topic you weren't prepared to discuss? What question might you have asked first?

Read: In Matthew 12:1–14, we find two instances of Jesus responding with questions. How did His question change the conversation?

Try: Practice the single question strategy for one day. Before you respond to anyone, ask them a question (even in everyday conversation). How do your conversations change?

Lesson 5

Wisdom and Compassion

When he saw the crowds, he had compassion for
them, because they were harassed and helpless,
like sheep without a shepherd. (Matt. 9:36)

Asking a question is also an opportunity for compassion, a quality that
should undergird our words in most hard conversations.

Much of the world operates under constant deception. People, like
sheep, are easily led astray. Challenges to the church's teachings may
arise from people who have never heard a biblical perspective on the
topic. It's no kindness to someone in need of Christ if we simply engage
that person in argument after argument—even if we know our topic
well and "win" every time. If we win a debate while ignoring a soul,
how does this honor Christ?

> ### If we win a debate while ignoring a soul, how does this honor Christ?

I once knew a man who routinely challenged me on the existence of
God. Initially, I mistook our discussions as an intellectual exercise. I'd
study for them and often felt I "came out on top." It took me a shame-
fully long time to clue in to their true nature. One day, exhausted, I
asked him, "Tom, you spend an awful lot of energy on this. Why is it so
important to you for God not to exist?"

His shoulders slumped, and his face became terribly sad. "Because
if God exists, it means He saw what my father did to my mom and me,
beating and abusing for years. It means He watched that and did nothing. It means He may love other people, but there's no way He loves me."

Our conversations changed radically after that. How I wish I'd utilized the single question strategy earlier.

Too often, we enter conversations focused on winning, proving our
point, providing answers, or defending the gospel. Of course, we want

to represent God well, but we know from the fact of Jesus's death on the cross that God doesn't need to "look like a winner" in every situation.

Compassion is no weakness (as demonstrated by Jesus) and doesn't have to weaken our position on what is true. But it can open our ears and guide us into asking more constructive questions and fashioning answers that don't sound like they came out of a dusty box of clichés stored in the church basement.

Even in hard conversations around death, hardship, or emotional situations, asking questions before offering counsel or answers can increase empathy and help us craft wiser, more effective encouragement. Jesus told his disciples to be "wise as serpents and innocent as doves" (Matt. 10:16). Wise questions inform hard conversations.

If we make a habit in all conversations to ask one or two questions before we respond, it helps destroy those initial walls we erect that truly serve no godly purpose. This often changes the nature of those discussions to something more in line with God's agenda. They may still be hard, but at least we'll be closer to a dialogue that makes a difference.

Suppose our colleague complains that we never cooperate with his ideas or projects. We might be tempted to respond immediately that we do cooperate, but too often, that would just engage us in an adult version of "No you don't!" "Yes I do!"

Instead, we might say, "I'm sorry you feel that way. Can you tell me what it would look like if I did cooperate with them? What would be different than things are now?" This diminishes our defensive wall and gives our colleague an opportunity to tell us what he needs. We may or may not be able to meet that need, but at least then we're having a conversation with real information.

Or perhaps our adult child comes to us and says she thinks we favor our other children over her. She believes we've never loved her the way we love the others.

We can instantly assure her that's not the case, or we can ask, "How would things look different in our family or in our relationship if we loved you equally?" This question allows her the chance to explain her perspective before we offer assurance, and our wall is clearly set aside to serve her. Maybe after listening, we can offer assurance in a more concrete way that she can feel.

Read a gospel in a single sitting, paying careful attention to how often Jesus responded to people with questions. He asked sick people if they wanted to be well. He asked disciples who they thought He was. He asked the Pharisees what they would do about healing on the Sabbath. Questions should be an integral part of a Christian's conversations, as they reflect the wisdom of our Lord.

> **Questions should be an integral part of a Christian's conversations.**

In my first job after college, I sat with the mother of two boys who'd run away from home. She wept and said to me, "I'm a bad mother. That's why they ran."

In my immaturity, I was quick to offer assurance. "I'm sure you're not a bad mom. Every parent feels that way."

She sniffed. "Thank you for saying that. My mom was mad at me for handcuffing the boys to their beds at night so I can go out with my new boyfriend, but she just doesn't understand that I need a social life to be a good mom. You understand, don't you?"

That's the moment I learned to ask, "What makes you think you're a bad mother?" before I put my stamp of approval on someone's parenting.

Asking a question before answering is valuable at the start of a conversation and throughout. It helps motivate the turtle, inform the hawk, and calm the chameleon. As this was His habit on earth, it also represents Jesus well.

Dismantling, descending, and immediately dismissing our internal walls clears the pathway for more constructive dialogues and creates opportunities to increase wisdom and compassion.

ARTwork

Answer: What important thing do you think others don't know about you because they don't ask?

Read: Matthew 21:23–27 tells the story of a time Jesus decided not to answer a question. How can this inform our guidelines for when to engage in a discussion and when to refrain?

Try: Good questions don't just appear from thin air. We must craft them. List questions you can ask others when a hard conversation arises and practice them. It can help to role-play potential hard conversations. We may learn something new about our friends or family by practicing questions. It can even spark a conversation to ask others if you can test your questions on them and get their feedback. God doesn't waste anything, even our practice.

HEART OF THE ART PRACTICE

Read Ephesians 2:14–22. Then, for the next week, don't change what you do in conversations, but keep a record of the times that either (a) you felt an impulse to speak, but didn't, or (b) you felt an impulse to listen, but didn't. Prayerfully examine your record for patterns.

Changing Lives

Changing Me, Changing You

Jesus looked at them and said, "With man it is impossible, but not with God. For all things are possible with God." (Mark 10:27)

Believing people can change is perhaps one of our greatest tests of faith. But if we're hoping to facilitate change in others, we must first believe that God can change us. Even when it comes to having hard conversations.

No matter what colorful metaphors I use to describe conversational barriers, they are daunting and real. Even after we've identified them, most of us need both strong incentive and powerful hope to address them. And the longer we've lived with ingrained patterns, the harder it may be to consider a change—unless, of course, we have proper motivation.

> **If we're hoping to facilitate change in others, we must first believe that God can change us.**

My dad has been a firefighter for over sixty-five years, a chief for over fifty-one. In those many decades of fire service, he'll say he learned the importance of embracing change. He's a role model in that he maintained curiosity and learned new skills right up to retirement at age seventy-nine. Of course, he didn't always recognize, independently, what changes were necessary until the right motivation appeared.

One night Dad's department responded to a call at the local assisted living center. There was a concern about toxic fumes, so residents evacuated. One Internet news outlet reported some of his firefighters hadn't taken appropriate precautions against hazardous materials. That wasn't true, so I called Dad to let him know.

"What? That information's wrong. What station is it on?" he asked.

"It's on the Internet, Dad."

He muffled the phone, but I could hear him shout to the firefighters, "Find the channel that has the Internet."

I raised my voice. "Dad, it's not television news. It's online. On the computer."

"What? The computer. No one cares about that. I'm not worried about computer news right now."

He hung up.

The next morning, I received a frantic call from Dad. "Lori Ann, I'm getting emails from across the country that my firefighters weren't wearing protective gear. Where are they getting this?"

I sighed. "That's what I tried to explain last night. Write these letters down and have your secretary find it on your computer."

Until that morning, he'd had no use for the Internet and so he felt no compulsion to learn to use it (much the way I initially felt about smartphones). The false reporting impacting his department's reputation, however, piqued his interest, and so, he educated himself. Now, he navigates the web with the best of us. His devotion to his department motivated his change. Our devotion to Jesus, the family of God, and those we're called to reach can motivate us to learn new habits of communication.

Despite what you hear on the streets or from the next pew, people can, and do, change. At all ages. We come to situations with distinct personalities, cultural and ethnic backgrounds, family dynamics, and life experiences, but we also all have the capacity for growth and change.

We don't all avail ourselves of this capacity. We aren't all willing to invest the work that growth requires, and certainly some transformations involve bona fide miracles from Jesus. But as Christians, there's no excuse for despair or hopelessness regarding the possibility of change.

In 2 Peter 1:5–8, Peter describes qualities that should be increasing in believers so that we can become fruitful and effective in our knowledge of Jesus. The teachings of the apostles make it clear that Christians are expected to continue changing more and more to resemble Jesus throughout our lives. Early in that same passage (v. 3), Peter assures us, "His divine power has granted to us all things that pertain to life and godliness." What better way to demonstrate God's power to change us than by being walking role models?

> **Despite what you hear on the streets or from the next pew, people can, and do, change.**

Jesus followers should be accustomed to seeing people improve (and being people who improve). Spiritual growth should be our standard procedure, character refinement de rigueur, and soul renovation a matter of course.

Every reader comes to this book from a different starting point. Even as I write, God knows who will read this page. He's aware of the challenges each faces regarding hard conversations. He is here with us. He welcomes all into the adventure.

When my son was young, he got agitated when cars passed us on the highway. "Mommy, hurry up. All those other people are winning."

"Zack," I'd say, "look behind us. There are cars there too. Do you remember a starting line? No. We're not in a race; we're on an adventure, and so are they. When others pass us, rather than worry, let's cheer for them instead." God was trying to teach me the same thing.

No matter where we begin, the life of a Jesus follower is a life of transformation ever toward the likeness of Christ. Paul says it this way in Romans 12:2: "Do not be conformed to this world, but be transformed by the renewal of your mind, that by testing you may discern what is the will of God, what is good and acceptable and perfect."

You may have a lifelong history of mouthing off too quickly and not listening. You may have spent decades keeping quiet when you should have spoken up. You're convinced you need to change, but you're unsure how.

Or you may embrace hard conversations and you're eager to improve. You see the value of challenging yourself to increased skills in this area.

Adversely, some of you may have bungled so many conversations, you reflexively warn people that you're socially awkward or prone to say the wrong thing in any situation. You know you want to improve, but everything you've tried just seems to backfire. You're willing to try again, but you have doubts about the hope of success in your case.

And a few of you still aren't convinced you're someone God even wants to have engaging in hard conversations. You're only reading this book to humor your spouse or because you were hesitant to make others uncomfortable by objecting to this choice for your small group. (Ah, you thought we didn't know you were here. Don't worry. We do.)

Everyone, inhale. Exhale. That's right. We're all going to be fine.

According to God's Word, we each have every hope of change, even if this book is the first time we've considered the need to do so. Jesus welcomes us even if we don't feel ready. It doesn't matter where we begin. It matters that we invite Him into the situation, by being open to the possibility that He has changes to make in us before (or as) He uses us in the lives of others.

ARTwork

Answer: What are you hoping changes in your life from reading this book? If you have only one effective hard conversation using these tools, which conversation would you want that to be and with whom?

Read: Luke 10:38–42 and John 11:17–27. Martha was on the receiving end of one of Jesus's famous hard conversations. In Luke 10, she's too distracted taking care of household details to pay attention to Jesus, but in John 11, we see a change. With a house full of mourners, Martha leaves everything to focus on Jesus the moment He draws near. How did that one hard conversation free Martha to focus on Jesus?

Try: See through God's eyes. When Jesus approached Martha, He made an observation that showed He'd already noticed her and understood something about her. Consider the one hard conversation you mentioned in answer to the first ARTwork question here. What have you observed about this individual? Pray for this person. Ask God to help you see what He sees.

Getting Up Again

But one thing I do: forgetting what lies behind and straining forward to what lies ahead, I press on toward the goal for the prize of the upward call of God in Christ Jesus. (Phil. 3:13–14)

But what if this is your third pass through this book? What if you've tried changing multiple times or you've mangled some situation because you didn't get this right? You're truly not alone.

Brenda sounded abrasive and uneducated whenever she spoke. This single mom had a special needs child who wasn't getting the help he needed, largely because Brenda didn't know how to communicate. Every conversation with professionals became a screamfest or worse, ended in threats of a police escort from their office. State officials threatened to remove her son from Brenda's care.

We sat at her kitchen table, and I asked, "Are you interested in understanding why people don't work with you?"

Punctuated with her usual flow of expletives, which I will not include here, she replied, "Of course I am. I'm willing to try anything to get my kid what he needs."

"Okay. Problem one is that when you speak, you sound angry and accusatory."

"I am angry. Why shouldn't I be angry? Anger gets results." (Again, insert your own exclamations.)

"How's that working out for you? Are you seeing these results?"

She squinted at me as she lit a cigarette. "No."

"All right then. Another problem, and I'm just going to talk straight with you because you talk straight with everyone else, yes?"

She nodded. "That's all I'm asking. Hit me with it."

"You absolutely know what you're talking about when it comes to your son. The problem is, you don't sound as if you know what you're talking about. In fact, you sound like the opposite of someone who knows what they're talking about. But I can help you learn to talk with people if you're willing to work. Change can be hard."

The mom slapped the table. "Can't be harder than watching my kid suffer without anyone listening to us. I'm up for it. Take me to school. I'll learn."

Our first step was a secret code. Whenever her volume rose, I gently tapped the table. When she saw the tap, she modified her tone, inhaled, and checked her language.

> If all you're adding to a conversation is volume, you're already down for the count. Tap out and regroup.

After a dozen or so times, she began to tap herself out of escalating conversations. One of the mottos we developed along the way is one I use often to remind myself to stay calm: "If all you're adding to a conversation is volume, you're already down for the count. Tap out and regroup."

She had little education, a long-standing pattern of uncouth speech habits, and a lifetime of trauma, but for the love of her son, she not only learned a new way to speak, but after a time, she also successfully advocated for him to have the supports he needs.

The other person in that story about change is me. When I began working with at-risk families as a twentysomething fresh out of college, I knew nothing practical. My method of communicating was mostly me talking and expecting others to absorb my pearls of wisdom and line up to change. Initially, helping others to change was a lot about my need to feel like a hero in other people's lives.

One night early on, I was leading a teen discussion group at an urban shelter. They rejected each of my carefully crafted topics until finally I said, "Look, I'm willing to talk about anything on your minds. Really. Choose a topic."

"Okay," said one young man, "let's talk about why you're so fat. What makes you eat more than you need?"

Taken aback, I replied, "Is that really what you want to discuss?"

"No," he said, smirking, "but we also aren't interested in your lame topics that have nothing to do with what's going on with us. It's like you don't listen. Plus, you think you have it all together, but at least most of us know when to put our forks down."

That was brutal (and he was rude), but it taught me lessons about listening and about acting as if I have all the answers. Before I could be a person who helped Brenda no matter how many times she had to start over, I had to be willing to be someone who kept trying no matter the number of failures behind me. There are people and situations that require persistent support to change. I'm one of those people, and learning to have hard conversations is one of those situations.

God patiently taught me through His Word, prayer, other people, and several decades of my own failures. Most of the lessons in this book were lessons I learned as Jesus picked me up off the mat. If you've made hundreds of mistakes trying to communicate with others, you're not alone. Don't stop trying. That's the only real path to failure.

ARTWORK

Answer: What are your reservations about trying new ways to engage in conversation? What is one way you'd encourage someone else facing the same reservations?

Read: The apostle Paul understood having to change to be like Jesus. Jesus transformed Paul from a zealous enemy of the church to an effective, fruitful apostle. Read Philippians 3:1–16. From where does Paul take his confidence?

Try: Memorizing Philippians 3:13–14 can be a valuable weapon against discouragement as we go forward. Try writing it on an index card and posting it on mirrors around your home or on the walls of your office until you can say it by heart.

Lesson 3

Faith—New and Renewed

Therefore, if anyone is in Christ, he is a
new creation. The old has passed away;
behold, the new has come. (2 Cor. 5:17)

Who doesn't get doubtful or discouraged after trying to change with little success? It's understandable to come to this huge topic of engaging in hard conversations with healthy skepticism. But God can take the most tenuous hope and weave it into a strong cord that becomes a lifeline for transformation.

Christians are sometimes guilty of making the life of a Jesus follower sound like a neat "before and after" situation, as if all of life just falls into place and our characters become perfect at the moment of our conversion. Most of us who have been in a lifelong relationship with Jesus can attest to the fact that following Jesus and becoming more like Him can be an arduous process.

> **God can take the most tenuous hope and weave it into a strong cord that becomes a lifeline for transformation.**

Following Jesus, though, is key. There's no hope of progress until you begin the journey. If you don't know Christ, I urge you to consider following Him today. Maybe you've struggled to change on your own (we've all been there). Jesus would like to provide you the strength and power to become a new creation, free from your past. Second Corinthians 5:17 says, "Therefore, if anyone is in Christ, he is a new creation. The old has passed away; behold, the new has come."

If you have a Christian in your life, find that person and say you'd like to follow Jesus too. Or pray right now. Romans 10:9–10 says, "Because, if you confess with your mouth that Jesus is Lord and believe in your heart that God raised him from the dead, you will be saved. For with the heart one believes and is justified, and with the mouth one confesses and is saved." In your own words, say this to God. Then, reach out to the Christian church or fellowship nearest you, and tell them you'd like support in your new journey.

Why is this so vital? There's an ancient Old Testament proverb that says, "There is a way that seems right to a man, but its end is the way to death" (Prov. 14:12). Without Christ, we're blind to destructive paths and practices that appear to be perfectly reasonable, but in fact, lead us to a place far from God.

Every Christian having hard conversations with other people started out having a hard conversation with God about the state of their own soul. God showed each of us (through His Word) how sinful we were and how helpless to free ourselves from this sinful state. He informed us that this sinful state would separate us from Him eternally without a remedy.

God demonstrated His love for us by sending His Son, Jesus, to die on the cross in payment for our sins. By acknowledging our need for salvation and accepting the salvation provided freely through Jesus's death and resurrection, we will never have to face separation from God.

A relationship with Jesus, though, isn't simply a deposit on a promise of eternity. We can live in the freedom God offers us for eternity right now. John 8:36 says, "So if the Son sets you free, you will be free indeed." Until Jesus comes again, we live in a fallen world, battling temptations and all manner of unseen forces, but Jesus provides a freedom to change that we can inhabit more and more as we grow up in our relationship with Him.

If you're a new believer, know that God accepts us where we are and provides deep pools of strength for change. When we start following Jesus, we don't become perfect. We become free to pursue God and all He has for us. Step into that freedom and embrace it as a lifelong process. Find mentors and role models for spiritual growth. Accept correction and direction. Request hard conversations so you can learn.

God's Word says, "Now the Lord is the Spirit, and where the Spirit of the Lord is, there is freedom. And we all, with unveiled face, beholding the glory of the Lord, are being transformed into the same image from one degree of glory to another. For this comes from the Lord who is the Spirit" (2 Cor. 3:17–18).

Maybe you've followed Jesus a long time but still struggle to change your speech, because even with Jesus and maturity, you're not feeling too confident learning new skills for hard conversations. Be assured you aren't the only one. We have hope for change right up to the day God calls us home.

Experienced believers can take great encouragement from the writer of Hebrews, who understood that pressing on toward growth in Christ means ongoing struggle, sacrifice, and endurance. This writer taught the value of keeping our eyes on Jesus through the long walk of obedience this life requires: "Therefore, since we are surrounded by so great a cloud of witnesses, let us also lay aside every weight, and sin which clings so closely, and let us run with endurance the race that is set before us, looking to Jesus, the founder and perfecter of our faith, who for the joy that was set before him endured the cross, despising the shame, and is seated at the right hand of the throne of God" (Heb. 12:1–2).

To say we can no longer change or grow is to say that the power of Jesus somehow diminishes the longer we walk with Him. Nothing could be further from the truth.

The more of our selves we surrender to Him, the greater the power at work in us and through us, so that we can say with John the Baptist, "He must increase, but I must decrease" (John 3:30).

ARTwork

Answer: Where are you in your walk with Jesus? What support do you need to deepen your relationship with Jesus?

Read: There are many "hard conversations" in Scripture, and Hebrews 12 is one of them. Read it several times and then write it in your own words. What verse or verses from this chapter apply to your current pursuit of learning the art of hard conversations?

Try: Invite a mature Christian friend, pastor, or spiritual mentor to share thoughts on ways you can continue to grow as a communicator for Christ. Tell that person you're hoping to expand your ability to engage in hard conversations and ask for prayer.

Lesson 4

Heroes and Saviors

*For there is one God, and there is one mediator
between God and men, the man Christ Jesus,
who gave himself as a ransom for all, which is the
testimony given at the proper time. (1 Tim. 2:5–6)*

When having hard conversations, keep in mind there is only one God and we're not Him.

Hard conversations are generally about initiating a change in view, character, behavior, or circumstance, often with eternal implications. It can be easy to lose perspective, to overstep, or to try to play the role of the Holy Spirit in others' lives.

Operating in a fallen world where temptations arise and forces of evil oppose us means there are many ways to go wrong when talking to others about change. One of those is trying to be the hero in someone else's story.

> **When having hard conversations, keep in mind there is only one God and we're not Him.**

Saffron was easily the most challenging person to whom I ever ministered. She was bright. She could be funny. She had a gentle heart. She also had serious mental health challenges that manifested in unreliable judgment and sporadically poor decision making. There were times when she listened through a hard conversation and relied heavily on my counsel. There were other times when she decided to toss great advice right out the window. I worked with her for years and we made great progress together. Sometimes, though, I forgot Saffron was responsible for her life, not me.

She reminded me of this during a particularly frightening period when she faced a lawsuit, one in which she was at risk of losing everything. Her opposition was unreasonable, but Saffron had little power in the situation. We attended a meeting with the plaintiff and Saffron's lawyer in which they made an offer I thought was quite a concession in an otherwise merciless situation. Saffron's lawyer advised her to accept the offer and I supported that. Back in my car, however, Saffron expressed serious doubts.

"I don't know what other choice you have, Saffron. It's not what you want, but at least it's something. Why hesitate?" I asked.

"You always tell me to think carefully about my decisions because I'm the one who has to live with them, don't you?" she replied.

"Well, yes, but—"

"Be honest. You wouldn't want to live with that offer. You're going home to your life tonight. So's my lawyer. If I take this offer, you feel like it's a win because it solves things for today, but I don't like what it looks like down the road. This is my life, my choice."

Don't rob people of the opportunity to be the hero of their own stories.

As I fumed at her reasonable argument, my own words floated back to me. Whenever I train anyone in helping others, I caution that person, "Don't rob people of the opportunity to be the hero of their own stories." Rejecting this offer wasn't a risk I would take, but it wasn't my risk, it was Saffron's. I did want the momentary win, but it would take something from Saffron.

Against all common sense, I yielded. We called the lawyer to explain that Saffron had opted to turn it down and face court. That night I prayed. I had little hope her decision was the right one, but I asked God for mercy. The next day, the other side delivered a new option that was beyond our wildest hopes. The lawyer and I were incredulous, but Saffron beamed.

"You always tell me that I'm the expert in my own life, Lori. Yesterday, it was like you forgot to believe that, but I didn't."

Our responsibility is to speak truth and to represent Christ in every hard conversation. It's the other person's responsibility to decide how to respond and what changes to make in response. Jesus is the only Savior anyone needs, and every person has a right to be the hero in an adventure with Him.

Another way we can go wrong is imagining that if we just do everything right, every conversation will have the outcome we desire.

I ran into a school social worker in the supermarket one day, and she seemed a little downhearted. "Is everything all right?" I asked.

"You haven't heard?" she said quietly. "Kwan is in the Adult Correctional Institution. He'll likely be there for several months."

My vision blurred with tears. Kwan and I had had countless conversations over the past several years. Many others had invested in him and offered him opportunities to make a better life than he'd been handed. It was truly disappointing to learn he'd chosen this path.

At home, I prayed. What different words could we have used? Was there someone else who might have gotten through to him? What did I miss? As I listened for God's answer, I thought of the prison and friends I knew in ministry there. Countless men and women behind bars had been on the receiving end of hard conversations they chose to ignore. Kwan wasn't alone.

Jesus was the perfect communicator, and many people turned away from Him unchanged. At the start of John 6, Jesus is surrounded by a multitude of listeners. By the end of the chapter, many disciples decide to walk away. It wasn't because He was a poor communicator. It's because He spoke truth and they didn't want to deal with truth.

No matter our efforts or expertise, we're wise to keep our expectations in check. Some hard conversations will result in fruitful change, while others will feel like dust in our faces. That doesn't mean they weren't effective. It just means they didn't meet our immediate expectations. Kwan is behind bars, but his story isn't over. Who knows when all the words spoken to him, like seeds, may sprout new life? He wouldn't be the first to find redemption during incarceration.

Maybe the conversations I had with Kwan will bear fruit in the lives of other workers who listened in or maybe in his younger siblings. Maybe God will use them to build some necessary quality in me. We don't always get to know.

The lessons in this book are about hard conversations, but they are also about faithfulness and persevering in speaking up without guarantees of desired outcomes, just as Jesus did when He walked here with us.

ARTWORK

Answer: What does it feel like when someone is using words to try to get you to change direction or behave in a way that doesn't interest you? How have you tried to manipulate others with your words?

Read: Read John 6. What can we learn about hard conversations from Jesus's response to many disciples walking away?

Try: Practice retroactive encouragement. Choose a night with friends to share stories about how many times they heard the truth about the gospel or about a behavior or characteristic before they decided to make a lasting change. Let these stories serve as a reminder that it can take multiple people speaking the same truth over time to penetrate the deception or willfulness of another's heart and mind.

Lesson 5

Foundation for Change

There is therefore now no condemnation for
those who are in Christ Jesus. (Rom. 8:1)

While on the face of it, changing ourselves and participating in the change of others can be daunting, God provides us with a solid foundation from which to operate. One college instructor used to tell us, "A Christian has nothing to prove and nothing to lose."

We have nothing to prove because we've already been found guilty, deserving of eternal separation from God, and yet we know that by grace we are saved through Jesus Christ. We have nothing to lose because our lives are sealed in Jesus (Col. 3:3–4) and we have no condemnation in Him (Rom. 8:1). This is the essence of the freedom we have in choosing to engage in the process of spiritual growth, both ours and others.

Not long after my first book was released (a book on Christian living and enduring hard times), I attended a party with people from a church I'd attended in my twenties. I was an immature Christian when they knew me and made many mistakes in their midst. At the party, one woman called me over and exclaimed enthusiastically about the book and its effect on her spiritual life.

She turned to the older woman sitting beside her and said, "I knew way back then that Lori would write a book that would impact the kingdom of God, didn't you?"

You have to give the older woman credit for blunt honesty, because she frowned, shook her head firmly, and replied, "Absolutely not. I never would have imagined."

I laughed because I understood. I wouldn't have believed it then, either, but by God's grace, I grew. I changed. So can we all.

Each of us in Christ, new believer to mature saint, operates from a secure foundation of God's stubborn, relentless love. Paul ends Romans 8 with powerful words: "For I am sure that neither death nor life, nor angels nor rulers, nor things present nor things to come, nor powers, nor height nor depth, nor anything else in all creation, will be able to separate us from the love of God in Christ Jesus our Lord" (Rom. 8:38–39).

We have nothing to fear from trying to improve at having hard conversations, speaking biblical truth, and attempting to deepen relationships, even knowing we will at times fail, make mistakes, or be ignored.

> **Giving up on growing up is a mistake when we have the promise of the Holy Spirit and a relentlessly patient Father to help us in our journey toward maturity and fullness in Christ.**

If the powers on Paul's list cannot separate us from God, neither can bumbling words, discomfort with confrontation, talking too much, or coming across as abrasive. Giving up on growing up is a mistake when we have the promise of the Holy Spirit and a relentlessly patient Father to help us in our journey toward maturity and fullness in Christ.

People can, and do, change. My father changed because of his love for his firefighters and their professional reputation. Brenda changed because of her love for her son. Saffron changed with the courage to make her own choices. I've changed through time in God's Word, multiple failures, and God's grace. Christians change, not under compulsion or guilt, but out of a love for Jesus and for others. This is our foundation and motivation for learning the art of hard conversations.

ARTWORK

Answer: What are some skills growing up or in your vocational life that took many attempts to learn or master? What kept you trying?

Read: Read 2 Corinthians 3:17–18 and rewrite it in your own words. Post it where you can meditate on it frequently as you read this book.

Try: Find a conversation code. When we've been in a long-standing pattern of poor communication, it can help to have a partner in change. Engage a close friend, coworker, spouse, or ministry partner in your change plan. When you've identified a pitfall, develop a simple signal your partner can send (an ear tug, throat clearing, touch on the arm) when you're falling into an old conversational pattern. It won't be long before you'll be tapping yourself out and enjoying a new, more effective habit.

HEART OF THE ART PRACTICE

Every personality can benefit from asking open-ended questions (questions that cannot be answered yes or no) before venturing an opinion or advice or before introducing new information to a conversation. Begin a list of open-ended questions that facilitate conversations you're most likely to encounter. Some examples follow.

What's your interest in knowing what the Bible says about that subject?

What words have others used that have comforted you in this time?

What are your hopes or goals for our conversation?

UNIT 5

A Time to Be Silent, a Time to Offend

Lesson 1

Answers or Arguments

So he questioned him at some length, but he made no answer. (Luke 23:9)

In every art, there's a place for silence. In music, it's called a rest. In visual art, it's called white space. Even in dance, there is a moment for the performer to stand still. In the art of hard conversations, there are times when it's right and in line with God's plan for us to stay silent. Consider some signs that silence may be in order, starting with people who are not really looking to engage in productive dialogue.

> **There are times when it's right and in line with God's plan for us to stay silent.**

Sometimes others aren't looking for answers, but arguments. They don't want resolution, but revolution. They're revved up and ready to take a shot at the next person who crosses their path. Don't be that person.

In one of my jobs, there was a woman who was unhappy with her family, most of whom were Christians. Whenever she returned from a weekend visit, she'd arrive at my desk loaded for bear. Usually, she'd greet me with a variation of the line, "Where do you Christians get off . . ." or "You Christians think you know everything. Well, let me tell you . . ." Before I knew about her family, we'd engage in a fruitless, circuitous debate. Once I understood her background, though, I greeted her rants with silent nods and an occasional question about her weekend until she wound herself down and was ready for a reasonable conversation.

> **When faced with someone who doesn't want to be bothered with the truth, silence can be a curative response.**

If a person is ranting and clearly needs to vent, it's usually not optimal or productive to meet that person on the "open field." When we're angry, excited, traumatized, or stressed, our executive function or ability to make reasonable decisions is diminished. When faced with someone who doesn't want to be bothered with the truth, silence can be a curative response.

A person may unleash a torrent of angry words. While it's tempting to meet the raving with equal force, the superior force is silence, with either steady, neutral eye contact or no eye contact (such as naturally results from busying ourselves with other work). If the other dares us to respond, the proper response is something like, "I have a response, but it's best for us both if I wait until we're calmer."

Similarly, on social media, it's wise to allow time to pass before responding to an angry comment or Facebook rant. Give the other person time to cool and allow yourself time to pray before typing words that may be viewed by a wider audience than you've ever imagined. We aren't required to respond to every rant aimed in our direction.

Jesus exercised this type of silence when faced with the angry mob who wanted to stone the woman caught in adultery. Read John 8:1–11 to watch how well it works.

Another effective strategy is one I call "obvious silence." Sometimes people bait us to debate, knowing full well our answers. This happens with skeptics, people who oppose our faith, or rebellious believers. They publicly goad us into reducing the gospel to bumper sticker answers or stating truth in a way that might cause others needless hurt.

In more dire situations, instances of severe persecution, others may set a snare trying to get us to either lie or expose ourselves to harm. These situations call for silence or a nonspecific but clear response such as, "I stand with Christ." Or "I believe what the Bible teaches."

I heard of an older missionary who was cornered by angry teens. They tormented him, goading him to quote Bible verses or "preach" to them. He remained silent and calm. He kept his eyes to the ground, not out of shame, but so as not to fuel their fire. He prayed silently for deliverance, which came when the teens bored of their game.

Proverbs 15:1 says, "A soft answer turns away wrath, but a harsh word stirs up anger." Jesus exercised this type of silence when facing His accusers on the night He was betrayed as described in Mark 14:53–65.

Sitting in total silence would be uncomfortable and impractical for most situations, but we can choose to stay silent on selective topics that arise. During a hard conversation, sometimes less productive or tangential topics are raised. If we attempt to chase all these rabbits down their respective trails, the conversation is likely to become either an exhaustive marathon or a fruitless folly.

When the other person is introducing numerous issues, acknowledge the issues generally but direct them specifically, as in "Wow, you've raised several important concerns, and there's no way to give them each the time they deserve right now. Let's set some of those topics aside for later, and see if we can make progress discussing X." (If the person expresses fear that you won't get back to the other topics, offer to write them down before focusing on the one.)

Planned ignoring is a similarly useful strategy. Immature individuals, people with mental health issues, teens, and/or combative persons may pepper a conversation with insults, accusations, unpleasant or unkind words, and unnecessary remarks. Sometimes these can be addressed through ground rules (behaviors agreed on prior to the conversation) or one firm reprimand, as in "I won't remain in active conversation with someone who insults me."

But we may try the "planned ignore" strategy to deflect attempts to derail the discussion. Don't address the bad conversational behavior. Instead, remain on topic. We'll know it's working when they reference what we're doing: "Hey, aren't you going to tell me to stop calling you that?" or "So, you don't hear me swearing at you?"

The proper reply is, "We're having an important conversation. I'm not willing to be distracted by what's unimportant in this moment."

ARTwork

Answer: When was the last time you engaged in ranting or venting about something? What helped you come to resolution?

Read: Nehemiah used this tactic when dealing with rumors in Nehemiah 6:1–14. Take a moment to read it and note Nehemiah 6:3: "And I sent messengers to them, saying, 'I am doing a great work and I cannot come down. Why should the work stop while I leave it and come down to you?'"

Try: Choose one of these "silent" tactics (obvious silence, selective silence, or a gentle answer) to use this week when you encounter someone looking for an argument. What is the result?

Lesson 2

Dangerous Personalities and Spirits

What have you to do with us, Jesus of Nazareth?
Have you come to destroy us? I know who you
are—the Holy One of God. (Mark 1:24)

John tells a story in his gospel about Mary anointing Jesus with an expensive ointment. It is at a dinner hosted by Martha in the home of Lazarus. It should have been a night of fellowship, but instead, Judas erupts in anger at Mary's use of the costly perfume: "But Judas Iscariot, one of his disciples (he who was about to betray him), said, 'Why was this ointment not sold for three hundred denarii and given to the poor?'

He said this, not because he cared about the poor, but because he was a thief, and having charge of the moneybag he used to help himself to what was put into it" (John 12:4–6).

How hurtful and disruptive this must have been for Jesus's hosts and friends. We've all been in a room where someone disrupted fellowship with hidden or unclear motives. Jesus doesn't engage Judas in a debate or ask him to share his opinion about stewardship and the poor. He sets a firm, protective boundary around Mary and ends the discussion.

Conversations with disturbed individuals can be circuitous and exhausting.

There are disturbed people wandering our world and sometimes sitting at our tables. It may be a result of mental illness, substance abuse, spiritual oppression, or strongholds of sin, but some are downright dangerous. Even when they don't present a physical risk, these individuals are emotionally taxing, as if they suck the air from a room. Conversations with disturbed individuals can be circuitous and exhausting.

We see an example of this in 1 Samuel 20:24–34 in a conversation between King Saul and his son Jonathan about David. Saul is intent on killing David. Jonathan doesn't want to believe it to be true, so as David hides, Jonathan observes his father's reaction.

Saul's rage would seem excessive to someone who doesn't know his underlying motive, and he won't give Jonathan a straight answer as to what David's done that offended him. Jonathan talked the king down from his plans once, but this conversation makes clear to him that the only action is to put distance between Saul and David. In other words, in his current state of mind, there's "no talking to him."

There may be "voices" in our conversations other than the ones we audibly hear.

Remember there may be "voices" in our conversations other than the ones we audibly hear. Sometimes those voices are spiritual forces, accusing us to one another or speaking lies to a person in the grip of darkness.

Other times they are voices a mentally ill person hears as clearly and loudly as they hear yours. And of course, there are the "tapes" that run in all our minds of things our mother or father, a former teacher, an abusive spiritual leader, or an unkind schoolmate may have said long ago that get triggered in a tense discussion, like invisible, but toxic landmines.

We must pray for discernment amid discussions. If we sense other forces (spiritual, emotional, mental, or substance-related) are at work and the conversation seems unusually unproductive, end it as quickly and firmly as possible.

Pausing a conversation may sound like the following comments.

"I don't mind intense conversations, but this one feels particularly unproductive right now. I'm going to ask us to stop here so we can pray and regroup. Let's plan to discuss it again at such-and-such a time."

Or "This is such an important topic, but I think our tone is becoming unproductive, and I can feel myself slipping into some very unbiblical attitudes. Let's agree to meet again on this, but I'd like to invite Pastor X to join us to help keep our conversation on target. Are you open to that?"

Or "I'm sensing your goal is to take us down a path I'm not willing to travel. We are going to have to end our talk here."

Step out of the situation to pray and obtain counsel. Sometimes prayer and fasting will result in a future breakthrough. Sometimes the person is locked, long-term, inside a tremendous force, and the only answer is to limit discourse, setting clear boundaries with the individual until there has been release or healing. (For example, "John, we've tried to talk this out numerous times with no success. I'm willing to have the conversation again, but only if you're willing to include someone capable of guiding us like a pastor or counselor.")

Decisions on setting these types of boundaries are rare, should not be made casually, and are best made with the counsel of a mature Christian pastor, leader, or trained Christian counselor. The enemy is the accuser. We shouldn't involve ourselves in accusing others of demonic strongholds or personality disorders. These conditions exist and do come into play in some situations, but when we suspect that's part of a conversational dynamic, we are wise to involve trained professionals in our assessments.

ARTWORK

Answer: When have you encountered someone who seemed intent on being negative or disruptive? What have you seen work with this person and what has made the disruption worse?

Read: In Mark 5:1–20, we see Jesus speaking—not with the man who was possessed, but with the demons who possessed him. A careful reading of verses 7–9 demonstrates that Jesus knew to address the spiritual forces controlling the man, not the man himself. Imagine trying to have a reasonable conversation with this man before Jesus delivered him. It would have been a waste of energy.

Try: Work on boundary-setting statements. In the moment of an encounter with a disruptive person, it's easy to lose perspective. It's helpful to prepare and practice some sentences that establish clear boundaries before our next encounter. Some examples follow.

"I'm happy to discuss this with you, but not if you're going to shout or call me names. If you do that, I'll take it as a sign that you'd like to table this conversation for later."

"This feels like gossip to me, and I'm uncomfortable continuing to discuss this with you. I'm sure it's not your intent, but nevertheless, we've fallen into it, so let's take another path."

"This is a serious subject for me. When you're joking and being sarcastic, I feel as if you're telling me you're not able to discuss this with the same respect I'm offering. I'm happy to discuss this whenever you're ready to do so without the casual attitude."

Lesson 3

Sometimes We Take the Hit

*So everyone who acknowledges me before
men, I also will acknowledge before my
Father who is in heaven, but whoever denies
me before men, I also will deny before my
Father who is in heaven. (Matt. 10:32–33)*

Just as we follow Jesus into silence, there are times we must follow Him into offense.

My mother's mother, Nana, was a colorful woman who enjoyed entertaining equally colorful guests. This entertainment sometimes grew loud and unruly. It was on a night when their living room was packed with laughing adults that my mom heard a male visitor proclaim God does not exist.

Mom was only fourteen. At thirteen she'd become a Christian and was already a serious student of God's Word. Mom felt compelled to defend her Lord. She entered the room of rosy adults and addressed the man. "You're wrong. There is a God. He does exist."

Nana crossed the room and slapped my mom hard in the mouth. "I've taught you better than to contradict adults. Apologize right now."

Stinging from the blow, Mom considered apologizing but remembered the passage she'd just learned from Matthew 10:33: "But whoever denies me before men, I also will deny before my Father who is in heaven." Emboldened by her blossoming relationship with God, she shook her head. "No. I won't apologize. God exists."

The evening didn't get any easier for Mom from there, but she wouldn't change anything about what she did. There are times, this side of glory, when there's nothing else to do but take the hit. There are times to simply state a truth you know will make the conversation harder, but it is an important truth to state nonetheless.

This is becoming more of an issue in our daily lives, especially our places of work. I was in cultural-sensitivity training at a former job. We had just applauded testimonials of staff who incorporated New Age sage-burning ceremonies or Native American sweat lodges into their work. One had invited dead relatives to attend a meeting to show respect for clients who engage in ancestor worship. This was all lauded as progressive and culturally accepting.

Suddenly, the mood in the room turned when a coworker told a story that distressed her. She described working with a family who emigrated from Central America. They'd insisted on calling their Christian clergy to pray with and discuss possible spiritual oppression by demons before having their teen assessed by a mental health professional.

There were tongue clucks and disapproving head shakes throughout the room. I hesitated, but then I raised my hand.

"Yes?" the instructor asked.

"What if the problem with their teen *was* spiritual demon oppression?"

"Very funny," she said, as others laughed with relief.

"I'm not joking," I persisted (with a boldness quite unlike me, I promise you). "We've discussed respecting all kinds of religious observances that others may consider suspect or void of purpose. Why aren't we respecting this family's belief system? What makes them the exception for our sensitivity?"

"Please tell me you're not suggesting demons exist?"

When I tell you every set of fifty-plus professionals' eyes were on me, please understand in that moment, I wanted to say, "Nah, just kidding. Forget I brought it up."

Instead, I replied, "The Christian Bible does teach the existence of angels and demons. Why would we disrespect that and yet invite long-dead ancestors to attend meetings without a thought?"

> **There will be times when no strategy, no question, no amount of active listening will change the fact that what we say is offensive to others.**

This statement didn't elevate my colleagues' opinions of me. It made me suspect. It made me appear less professional. I imagine there was some conversation behind my back during lunch break. I care about that, but I care about the truth more (only by God's grace). Practicing simple ways to state the facts of our faith is becoming increasingly crucial in a culture quite comfortable telling us we're wrong.

Jesus pulled no punches when He warned us of the by-product of truth: "And a person's enemies will be those of his own household. Whoever loves father or mother more than me is not worthy of me, and whoever loves son or daughter more than me is not worthy of me. And whoever does not take his cross and follow me is not worthy of me. Whoever finds his life will lose it, and whoever loses his life for my sake will find it" (Matt. 10:36–39).

Hard verses, but ones we must heed as we engage in hard conversations. There will be times when no strategy, no question, no amount of active listening will change the fact that what we say is offensive to others.

The gospel is offensive. The truth that there is only one way to God—through Jesus Christ—is exclusionary. A biblical view of sin is in direct opposition to many modern lifestyles. People will accuse us of hatred, violence, intolerance, and hypocrisy for saying so, even if we say it nicely. But it's often love's job to say the hardest thing.

▎ It's often love's job to say the hardest thing.

Mark tells the story of Jesus's encounter with a rich young ruler. This man appears to earnestly seek eternal life. He kneels before Jesus and asks what he must do to find it.

Jesus tells him to keep the commandments, and the ruler assures him he's done so since his youth. The next line impressed me deeply from the first time I read it: "And Jesus, looking at him, loved him, and said to him, 'You lack one thing: go, sell all that you have and give to the poor, and you will have treasure in heaven; and come, follow me'" (Mark 10:21).

Did you catch that? Jesus looked at him, loved him, and then told him the hardest thing he could have heard. We know how hard it was because the man, disheartened, walked away sorrowful, because he had many possessions.

Sometimes there will be no other path for our conversations to take, except division. Employ every tool in this book, press in deep to Jesus, invest hours of prayer, and still, sometimes we'll find ourselves with a slap across the face, a suspect reputation, a lost promotion, a divided ministry team, or a loved one who walks away. It's out of love that I warn you of this hard thing.

There's no *but* at the end of this lesson. It's just important we remember such things.

ARTWORK

Answer: When have you stood up for a biblical truth and faced rejection for it? What did you learn?

Read: Read Matthew 10 several times. How can the warnings Jesus gave His disciples inform the way we conduct ourselves in our times?

Try: Use redemptive speech. During hard conversations, Christians are sometimes accused of being negative. This is a hard charge to avoid when confronting someone on sin, discussing the consequences of not following Christ, or helping loved ones face hard truths. I, for one, struggle with "being positive," especially when it feels forced or manufactured. However, I'm not by nature a negative person. Informed by my relationship with Jesus, I am a hope-filled person, and this is what I attempt to bring to all my conversations.

We can do this by focusing not on using positive or negative language but on using redemptive language. Redemptive language consists of words and messages that are direct, biblically informed, loving, truthful, and yet, always hopeful. It may sound like the comment below.

"The prognosis from the doctor is grim. If it weren't for Jesus, I would feel I was without hope. But Jesus has the final word on my life, not the medical world. So, I'll prepare for the future they predict, but I'll pray for the future I desire."

Or look at the following comment.

"What you've done to your marriage, family, and church through this adultery is serious. We'll likely experience the effects of those poor choices for years. However, God is great and merciful, your repentance is sincere, and if you're willing to continue to make hard choices and reparations, who knows what God may bring about? He isn't done with any of us yet."

Lesson 4

Take Space

*And he lay down and slept under a
broom tree. (1 Kings 19:5)*

In 1 Kings 18, we read of a time when Elijah demonstrated heroic faith in God by taking on the priests of Baal and literally calling down fire from heaven. He then destroyed these false prophets and prayed to God for rain. This was a powerful time in the life of the prophet, and God had mightily used Elijah. The consequence, though, was that Queen Jezebel determined she would hunt Elijah down and take his life.

So, in the very next chapter, following acts of faith and miracles of fire and rain, we find the prophet on the lam from a murderous regent asking God to take his life: "But he himself went a day's journey into the wilderness and came and sat down under a broom tree. And he asked that he might die, saying, 'It is enough; now, O LORD, take away my life, for I am no better than my fathers.' And he lay down and slept under a broom tree" (19:4–5).

Sometimes silence is the proper practice because we're the ones out of sorts.

God's answer to Elijah? He let him sleep. He sent ministering angels with food and water and let him sleep again. God is God and we are not Him. We grow weary and when we do, we are apt to say things that are not characteristic of who we are. Sometimes silence is the proper practice because we're the ones out of sorts.

There are days after working with crisis situations that I'm so weary, I spend the evening in silence, or I'd be picking fights with others. This is an especially important caution for good communicators. When we're overtaxed, unwell, or in a poor frame of mind, our words can become weapons too often aimed at those closest to us. Make a practice of taking "silence breaks." These can be as refreshing as coffee or a quick swim.

Of course, it's important to clue our loved ones in to why we need these breaks. Talk with those closest to you (when you're not weary) and explain there may be times you need to rest or tune out in order to be your best with them. Be careful not to make a habit of running out of steam for your inner circle, though. It's not fair to spouses, children, roommates, or parents if we spend all our energy communicating well with others, but all they encounter is someone who needs silence or rest.

In fact, these loved ones may have more insight than we do about what the signs are that we need a break. Ask them or your assistant, office mate, or best friend what they see when they know you would benefit from a break. It can also be helpful to give them permission to tell you when those signs appear.

When my children were small, I taught them how important it was for Mommy to spend time with God every day to be the best mommy I could be. One day when I was particularly grumpy, Zack brought me my Bible and my coffee mug. In a stage whisper, he told me, "Here, Mommy. I'll watch Hannah for a few minutes. I think you need a little more time with God today."

If you're midconversation when you feel your attitude and tone slipping and realize you need a break, own it. Say something like, "I need us to pause here. You're raising important issues and I'm not giving you my best right now, but you deserve that. If it's all right with you, I'd like to take a rest and then we can pick this up again in two hours. Okay?"

Our cars can be sanctuaries during workdays (silence the radio and phone) for quick breaks. Noise-canceling headphones can be an oasis in a busy office or school setting. Sometimes taking a quick walk around the block provides all we need. At home, enjoy your yard, porch, rooftop, or nearby woods, park, or water. In strenuous seasons, plan entire days of silence. Unplug to recharge. In Mark 6:30–32, Jesus pulls the disciples away from the crowds to rest.

As followers of Christ, we do well to follow Him as readily into silence as we do into conversation. Remember, in the power of Christ, silence can reach a soul as readily as a shout.

ARTwork

Answer: Describe a time when silence played a positive role in your life.

Read: Study any (or all) of the passages mentioned in this unit for the ways Jesus or other biblical figures utilized silence. Consider there were four hundred years of God's silence between the Old and New Testaments. What was the purpose of that silence?

Try: Do no harm. Silence is a worthy conversational tool, but like any tool, it can also be a weapon. Christians are to act in love, truth, and kindness. Silence should never be used as a punishment (as in "giving someone the silent treatment"), as a coward's refuge (as in "I knew I should speak up for that coworker being bullied at work, but I need this job"), or as an escape (as in "Whenever people open their mouths about faith, they wind up in troublesome conversations, so I just stay out it").

Silence is a powerful conversational gift and should be used with respect, love, and restraint. A version of silence that we can use liberally, especially in our homes, is to lower our volume. The world has become a place of much yelling and sometimes that seeps into our homes. Speak softly, use fewer words, and be direct for one week. You may be surprised how much better you're heard.

HEART OF THE ART PRACTICE

Read Romans 8. List people who inspire you to improve your skills at hard conversations. Maybe it's someone close to you—a parent, spouse, child, or other family member. Maybe it's coworkers, teammates, or fellow servicemen and servicewomen. It could be an entire group like your congregation, a tribal people, or high schoolers. Maybe it's Christ alone. Whoever it is, pray daily for God's heart for that person or people.

PART 2

Prepare for Success

UNIT 6

Where Is the Path to the Point?

Heart Condition

*The good person out of the good treasure of his
heart produces good, and the evil person out of his
evil treasure produces evil, for out of the abundance
of the heart his mouth speaks. (Luke 6:45)*

Imagine you've been invited to dine with a friend. You arrive to find a table set with fine china, expensive silverware, crystal so clear it's nearly invisible, an ornate candelabra with glowing tapers, and a centerpiece of the most delicate roses. The air is scented with lavender. To one side, a three-piece orchestra plays chamber music, and the view overlooks the ocean. It's a starry night and harbor lights dance on the waves.

The food arrives, but when you look at your plate, it's raw chicken, bad fish, blighted potatoes, and moldy kale. The waiter pours water into your glass, but it's cloudy and smells like high tide. The cream is sour.

When you hesitate to tuck in, your host expresses dismay and points out all the trouble he's taken to create the perfect setting. You acknowledge the effort, but stare at the food, wondering why anyone would imagine that ambiance and delivery could make this rotted food and fetid water palatable. In fact, the impeccable setting only adds a surreal disorientation to the experience.

Similarly, all the conversational skills in the world cannot make the words of a self-serving or corrupt heart nourishing to anyone's soul. A heart yielded to Jesus inherits His righteous goodness, but we can harbor bad attitudes, precious sins, and old habits that affect its outpouring.

> **No matter what . . . words emerge from our mouths, it's the condition of our hearts that brings effectiveness and fruitfulness to the table.**

No matter what tenor, quality, order, or tone of words emerge from our mouths, it's the condition of our hearts that brings effectiveness and fruitfulness to the table. No matter how soft the office sofa, how sweet the coffee, or how wide the smiles, without the right attitude individuals can emerge from hard conversations utterly crushed in spirit and confused as to why.

Contrast that confusing meal with the first Thanksgiving hosted by my daughter and her new husband, the chef. They phoned me an hour before our scheduled arrival to request a pound of butter. I delivered the emergency supply and noticed my daughter wasn't dressed for company, the tables weren't set up, and their tiny kitchen was in disarray.

As more family arrived, offers of assistance were waved off as our hosts took their time setting up borrowed tables, mismatched place settings, and glasses that had once served as canning jars. This mama was a tiny bit nervous about the meal.

My nerves were completely misplaced. The butter wasn't a forgotten item, but the *fifth* pound used in the delicacies we enjoyed that day. Each dish they set on the table was richer and more delicious than the first. The newlyweds tended to and waited on all of us with sensitivities to favorite tastes, dietary restrictions, and special needs from the youngest to the oldest.

We ate until we burst and requested to-go containers for the rest. Their relaxed attitude and attention to relationship over presentation was infectious. That meal was a feast of comfort food, family, laughter, and love despite the imperfect timing and mishmash of tables and settings.

Many of us brace for rejection and failure before hard conversations.

Fewer of us prepare for success. These next units provide tools for that endeavor. Preparation can increase the effectiveness of both planned and spontaneous hard conversations, but that groundwork begins in our own hearts and souls.

This book contains strategies for navigating challenging conversations. However, if you employ them all but neglect the condition of your heart, they will simply become tools in the hands of the enemy. If you forget a new skill, even your bumbling, fumbling, halting, hesitant words can become a feast for other souls, if you allow Christ to continually refresh and renew your heart by His Word and the work of His Holy Spirit.

> **Many of us brace for rejection and failure before hard conversations. Fewer of us prepare for success.**

Hard conversations backfire or detonate lives because the people engaged in them haven't applied the necessary soul-work prior to opening their mouths. Jesus described this problem with a parable in Luke 6:39–42.

> He also told them a parable: "Can a blind man lead a blind man? Will they not both fall into a pit? A disciple is not above his teacher, but everyone when he is fully trained will be like his teacher. Why do you see the speck that is in your brother's eye, but do not notice the log that is in your own eye? How can you say to your brother, 'Brother, let me take out the speck that is in your eye,' when you yourself do not see the log that is in your own eye? You hypocrite, first take the log out of your own eye, and then you will see clearly to take out the speck that is in your brother's eye."

This passage is frequently misapplied. In turtle mode, we use it to justify never speaking up while we languish in a continual process of half-removing logs from our own eyes. In hawk mode, we use it as a shield to deflect or dismiss any hard conversations directed at us, implying that every confronter remains log-laden.

Jesus intended this parable not to silence or to shield us but to provide us with guidance for the process of interacting with one another. It's how serious Christians grow into the kinds of good trees that produce fruit, as we see in the verses that immediately follow in Luke 6:43–45.

> For no good tree bears bad fruit, nor again does a bad tree bear good fruit, for each tree is known by its own fruit. For figs are not gathered from thornbushes, nor are grapes picked from a bramble bush. The good person out of the good treasure of his heart produces good, and the evil person out of his evil treasure produces evil, for out of the abundance of the heart his mouth speaks.

Wouldn't it loosen the tongue of more turtles to have the Christ-centered confidence that we were speaking from the abundance of hearts transformed by Him? And wouldn't people welcome hawks if what came swooping toward them could be trusted to emerge from the same abundance?

ARTwork

Answer: Think of a challenging conversation you've initiated that ended well. What was the condition of your heart toward that person prior to the chat? What did you do spiritually to prepare?

Read: Read Psalm 19 in your favorite Bible translation. Rewrite it in your own words, meditating on its meaning as you do.

Try: Rehearse. It can help you identify heart issues you may need to address first within yourself to role-play your conversation with another mature believer. It also allows you to work out what you plan to say and receive feedback from a sympathetic listener.

Ask the other person to assume the role of your listener and then role-play your conversation. Set a timer for ten minutes. Ask for feedback when time is up.

Rehearsal is useful when you're preparing to testify to someone about your faith experience, deliver hard news, encourage or exhort another believer, or have a heart-to-heart with a friend. With confrontations over specific sin, it's important to follow Matthew 18:15–17, so this would exclude a rehearsal with a proxy prior to taking the first step in the process, but rehearsal may be useful in preparing if the second step is necessary.

Even if no one is available, you can rehearse alone in your office, home, or car until you're comfortable and can speak naturally.

Lesson 2

Training Day

For while bodily training is of some value, godliness is of value in every way, as it holds promise for the present life and also for the life to come. (1 Tim. 4:8)

Depending on your personality, you may experience mild frustration in the next pages because it will feel like an unnecessary delay on the way to those conversations you're eager to accomplish.

It's not. This is the path. It isn't easy or quick, but few things worthwhile are. God drove that home to me through a former teacher—not a Bible teacher, but a martial arts instructor.

In my forties, I studied karate, eventually earning my black belt. One black belt was a stern instructor. During our warm-ups one afternoon, he instructed us to hit the floor for two hundred push-ups. A newer student complained, "Oh sure, easy for you."

He stopped class with a wave of his hand and scowled. "You know what?" he said. "I hear that kind of statement all the time. And I'll give you this—two hundred push-ups are easy for me, but do you know why?"

No one dared answer, so he continued. "Before any of you are awake, I start my day with double the exercises we'll do this entire class. After breakfast, I train several hours more. I discipline my mind, spirit, and body with proper hydration, food, and sufficient sleep. I've done this for over twenty years. Would you like it to be easy for you too? Quit whining about the first two hundred push-ups and get to work."

> **Grace is free; growth follows an investment of attention to Christ and application of His truth.**

We apply discipline, training, and effort to all manner of worthwhile pursuits—the arts, sports, careers, homes, gardens, hobbies, and entertainment. Why would we imagine we wouldn't have to be intensive about our training in the ways of Jesus Christ? Grace is free; growth follows an investment of attention to Christ and application of His truth.

Using any concordance, you'll discover the word *miracle* appears in the Bible significantly fewer times than "work," "build," "labor," "battle," "trust," and "faith." So why do we lose heart or wonder where God is when the miracle appears less often than the opportunity for hard work, spiritual battle, and faith? We rely on grace for our salvation, but we apply effort in our pursuit of becoming like Christ. That effort takes many forms.

Reading, studying, and meditating on Scripture, prayer, worship, giving, fellowship with believers, and service are foundational disciplines for soul training. Other disciplines include submission (yielding what we desire to what God desires), solitude (for reflection), fasting (both from food or from other things such as social media that can become idols), and engaging in Sabbath rest.

If our desire is to be like Jesus in our words and conversations with others, we study the Master. Just as in karate, when our best teacher is one who has achieved a high rank, so it is with this. We study Jesus. We invite mature believers to provide us feedback on our efforts. We seek role models who are effective in relationships and discipleship.

One of this sensei's pet peeves was people who train without using the correct form or technique. "You've just made achieving the proper form a thousand times harder for yourself by training this muscle incorrectly," he'd chide. Then he'd demonstrate the proper technique for a block, kick, or punch.

Many of us face a similar challenge when it comes to having productive conversations. We have spent years exercising our conversational muscles without any thought to proper form, so now the work of correction and development is harder. How much easier is it to learn and practice healthy lifestyle habits from our youth rather than trying to employ them once a life-threatening condition develops? It becomes harder as we grow older. Hard, yes. Impossible? Not in relationship with Jesus.

ARTWORK

Answer: What are some bad speech habits (interrupting, complaining, gossiping) you have that need to be replaced by healthier, more biblical practices? List a replacement for each (for example, reflecting on what another says before responding, expressing gratitude instead of complaining, evaluating whether it's constructive to talk about someone else and their behavior).

Read: In 1 Corinthians 2:1–5, Paul describes his approach to proclaiming Christ. Where is his focus if it's not on the words? What implication does this have for us?

Try: Use the crime show model of conversation. Anyone who watches crime shows or reads mystery novels knows that we generally don't find out why the culprit did what he did until the very end. We can take a clue from this ourselves when having hard conversations, rather than asking "why" questions such as "Why did you make that decision?" "Why won't you stop that behavior?" or "Why do you think you can't stop being sad?" Seek a different path.

We make better conversational and relational progress by asking "who, what, when, where, and how" questions. "Whose advice did you consider in making that choice?" "What happened in your life just before you made that decision?" "When was the last time you considered changing that behavior?" "How is that behavior affecting you or others around you?" "Where have you looked for support in handling your grief?" These types of questions provide information, often grounded in observable facts rather than vague guesses at "why."

And any fan of crime shows or mysteries will tell you that once we've answered who, what, when, where, and how, we can often answer the why on our own.

Heart-Work Behind the Artwork

*For if you keep silent at this time, relief and
deliverance will rise for the Jews from another
place, but you and your father's house will perish.
And who knows whether you have not come to the
kingdom for such a time as this? (Esther 4:14)*

The best preparation for knowing when to speak up or when to remain silent is to live in tune with the Holy Spirit. Sometimes a moment appears and will be lost if we don't act. Other moments call for restraint.

First Peter 3:15 commands this: "But in your hearts honor Christ the Lord as holy, always being prepared to make a defense to anyone who asks you for a reason for the hope that is in you; yet do it with gentleness and respect."

If you're a Christian but aren't prepared to give a reason for your hope, seek counsel from a trusted, mature Christian teacher or counselor. This is a common situation, easily rectified. Your answer can be as simple as one sentence, but God wants us to have a response ready that we can share with gentleness and respect.

> **God never leaves nor forsakes us. He is present to supply words in any situation.**

One happy by-product of being sure we know this answer is that we can respond when our own hearts ask us the reason for our hope. It's a defense against doubts that can assail any of us. So, doing the work of being prepared serves a purpose within us, even in situations that call for us to remain silent.

As we address the preparation that usually precedes a productive exchange of words, remember that the Holy Spirit can, on occasion, override the need for this prep and provide everything we need in a heartbeat. God never leaves nor forsakes us. He is present to supply words in any situation. Learning to know and obey His voice is foundational for hard conversations and for life.

The Bible also describes special circumstances for the body of Christ regarding words. When Jesus taught His disciples about signs of the end of the age, He issued this warning and a promise: "And when they bring you to trial and deliver you over, do not be anxious beforehand what you are to say, but say whatever is given you in that hour, for it is not you who speak, but the Holy Spirit" (Mark 13:11).

All Christians can be assured that if we are present for the times Jesus describes, God will provide us with verbal manna. We won't devote time addressing what to say in circumstances of severe persecution because God promises to give us words in those moments. We can trust Him fully to do as He promises.

So then, what exactly goes into earnest preparation?

I've found it useful to prayerfully consider six key questions prior to any hard conversation. For ease of reading, I'm going to use the singular word *person*, even though some of us are addressing groups of people. The preparatory questions are the same whether speaking to one or many.

As a word of encouragement for readers eager to "just get on with the work," let me assure you these questions take longer to explain than they do to utilize. Sometimes I spend days mulling over them. Other times they flip through my mind like a news ticker on a television screen, and the process of preparing is over in a flash.

God called Queen Esther to have a hard conversation that could have cost her life. In the balance for this conversation were the lives of her people, the Jews. She, her women, and all her people prepared for three days prior to her meeting with the king.

Alternately, Jesus often doesn't appear to take any time to prep prior to His hard conversations, but we know from Scripture He made a habit of rising while it was still dark or withdrawing to desolate places to pray. Jesus prepared daily because He understood that every one of His conversations would have eternal implications. I suggest we adopt this same attitude.

By making the questions a habit, we develop a lifestyle of aligning with God, listening to and loving others, and removing logs from our eyes before words emerge from our mouths. It may feel burdensome initially, but like new recruits at boot camp, we can trust that what feels unwieldy, awkward, and impossible now, will, with time and practice, become second nature.

Here is the complete list. We'll address each in depth, jumping right into question one in the next lesson:

1. What's my point?
2. What do I know about the other person?
3. What emotions may be involved in this conversation?
4. What biblical guidelines exist for this conversation? (Is it based in truth?)
5. Is this conversation grounded and timed in love?
6. What's my plan for following up either success or rejection?

ARTwork

Answer: How do you prepare for hard conversations now? What do you consider before initiating a tough talk?

Read: When Queen Esther had to gather her courage for the hardest conversation of her life (Esther 4), she not only prepared, she asked the other Israelites to prepare with her. What did she ask of them and what can we learn from her method?

Try: Set up preparation pages. When you're agitated about a situation but unsure if you should speak up, try this. Set a timer for five minutes every day for five days (in the morning or at bedtime) and write about your agitation without stopping. Try to fill several pages in each sitting. It doesn't have to make sense. You can repeat yourself. You will show these pages to no one, so write freely.

Wait the day (or overnight), and then reread the pages and circle phrases that recur, points you may need to research biblically, and sentences that may reflect an area of prayer for your own heart. This process will serve to (a) reduce obsessive thinking about the situation, (b) help you get to the bottom of your own agitation, and (c) clarify for you the points that may require a conversation.

Lesson 4

What's My Point?

Then the king said to me, "What are you requesting?" (Neh. 2:4)

The most productive hard conversations begin with us talking to God. That's what we've surveyed in the last three lessons. Once your heart is focused on Christ and you've invited Him to examine your motives and your attitudes, you're ready to prepare to include another human in the conversation. Let's take a look at question one.

What's my point?

It's a simple enough question. Probably not surprising that you should know what you want before you begin a hard conversation. What is surprising is how few people do. Like my friend Paul.

Several people sat trapped around the table as Paul launched into a high-volume tirade about how he wasn't going to stand for our kind of help anymore.

"I've had it with all of you. Done. You're supposed to help me, and instead, all I get is what I've always heard all my life. None of you understands me. If you can't care about me, I don't even want to look at any of you. I need help, don't get me wrong. I'm not saying I want you to leave. I'm not saying you're not helping. I'm not saying I'm quitting."

I held up my hand. "Paul, you clearly feel strongly about something. Instead of telling us what you aren't saying, what if you just make your point?"

"My point?"

"Yes. What do you hope changes because of our conversation?"

As it turned out, Paul was simply tired of hearing of one person's focus on the value of anger management. This was simple enough to address, and we were able to move on. It required a much longer discussion than would have been needed if he had been prepared with his point.

The first key question you'll want to consider before initiating a hard conversation is: What's your point? It sounds obvious, but all of us have had the experience of hearing someone natter on with great passion, even biblical messaging, only to wonder what exactly they're trying to say (if you're reading this in a group, don't everyone look at the most frequent offender at once).

In Nehemiah 1–2, Nehemiah provides a stellar example of the value of knowing your point. Upon hearing of the sorry condition of Jerusalem, Nehemiah had a passionate and visceral reaction. Here was a man in daily contact with the king and yet, before opening his mouth about a deeply felt need, he fasted and prayed. In this way, when the king finally asked him what he wanted, he had a coherent answer.

> **A plain, precise point can prevent confusion and promotes concrete progress toward a shared purpose.**

Conversations are more likely to be effective when we begin knowing what we want. Before you initiate a hard conversation, ask yourself precisely what you feel needs to be addressed with this person (or people), why, and what would be the ideal outcome for your conversation. A plain, precise point can prevent confusion and promotes concrete progress toward a shared purpose.

Clearly state (or write) your answer. Be honest. Imagine you'll never show this preparatory work to anyone. (In fact, feel free to shred it.)

Once you've written your point, shorten it to as few words as possible. This not only helps prepare your words, but it also clarifies your thinking. Clear thoughts are a boon in hard conversations. Some people take what they've written and bring it as a prompt or a reminder, but others just use it to home in on their primary focus.

Remember, write what needs to be addressed, why, and what your ideal outcome looks like to you. Several examples follow:

- "I have to tell my children I've been diagnosed with cancer. I don't want them to hear it from others, and I want to help them process what's about to happen to our family. It's important they know I'm still here for them and that we can trust Jesus even now. I hope at the end of this conversation, they feel at peace with the truth and know they can still enjoy being children while I go through treatment."

- "I'm angry with my pastor. He didn't choose me to run vacation Bible school this year. I thought I did a great job last year, but apparently, he didn't. I want to understand why he didn't choose me, and I want him to know it hurt my feelings that he didn't tell me he chose someone else. I hope that in this conversation he acknowledges he could have handled the situation better. I also hope I no longer feel unappreciated and we work together better in the future."

- "My father isn't a Christian. I want to be sure he has a clear understanding of what it means to have a relationship with Jesus. He's getting older, and I'm afraid he'll die without salvation. My dream is that because of our conversation, he either decides to accept Jesus right there or becomes curious and is willing to have more conversations."

- "My friend has decided to leave her husband to move in with a woman. I want her to know how much I love her and care that she's in pain, but that I can't support this choice. I hope that through our conversation, my friend feels loved. I'd be thrilled if somehow it was the start of her changing direction toward repentance, but if not, I hope it helps explain the uncomfortable dynamics that may be present in our friendship going forward."

- "My coworker constantly complains about Christians and makes derogatory remarks about my faith. I want him to know I respect his right to have his own views on Christianity, but his daily insults bother me. At the very least, I hope this stops his commentary, but beyond that, I hope it opens a spiritual dialogue."

- "I'm concerned about how much my Christian daughter is drinking. In practically every photo of her on social media, she's holding a glass of wine. I don't want to come across as legalistic, and I don't want to make her feel awkward around me, but there's alcoholism in our family tree. I hope it's not a problem for her, but I want to tell her how uncomfortable I am seeing her drink so often. I hope the way she responds reassures me that it hasn't become a problem and that she's more thoughtful about this choice. I also hope to see fewer photos of her drinking."

- "When my husband apologizes to guests for our home or the food we're serving, it embarrasses me, and I feel as though he's putting me down. Most of our friends are better off than we are, so I know he's just uncomfortable with our modest offerings, but it hurts me and I want him to stop."

- "One of my friends is going through a terrible time of poor health. I never know what to say in situations like this. I'm afraid of saying the wrong thing, but he's important to me. I want to be in this with him in any way I can—praying, talking, listening, whatever he needs—and I want him to know he's important to me. I hope from our conversation, he feels comfortable giving me specific ways he would feel supported."

Stating or writing our point clearly is the first step in sorting through what can often be a flood of words and feelings surrounding a hard topic. Brevity leads to clarity. Clarity leads to calm.

Brevity leads to clarity. Clarity leads to calm.

Work to state your point in as few words as possible. Proverbs 10:19 says, "When words are many, transgression is not lacking, but whoever restrains his lips is prudent." This process can help us manage powerful emotions and stray thoughts that might complicate or confuse matters. Furthermore, it provides us a starting place for measuring the effectiveness of our discussion.

ARTWORK

Answer: Think of an occasion when someone approached you with a potentially hard conversation, but you could address the concern quickly. Did that person use many words or few to introduce the point of the conversation?

Read: Read Nehemiah 1–2 and note what steps went into his preparation for his hard conversation with the king.

Try: Write the point you'd like to make in the same pattern as the examples in this chapter, then whittle the point down to three sentences. Then two. Can you do one?

HEART OF THE ART PRACTICE

Technological Hawk Support

Technology can be a hawk's best friend. We can't always have a partner in the room for our conversations, but we can set our own subtle reminders. Before your next conversation, set your phone or watch to beep or vibrate every five minutes. If you're speaking every time it sounds, you still have significant work to do around listening.

Allow the alarm to prompt you to pause and ask the other person to speak. Have some transitions ready: "I've been speaking, but I'd love to hear any thoughts you're having right now." "Give me a window into your perspective on this topic, won't you?"

When you reach a point that you aren't always the one speaking as the alarm goes off, you can know you're improving at sharing the conversational airspace.

I Hope I'm Wrong, a Phrase for Turtles

A nonthreatening way to confront another person with a concern is to lead with the idea that you may have the situation wrong and if so, you want to be corrected. This sounds like, "John, I hope I'm wrong, but it feels as though you want me to join you in gossiping about the pastor right now. What is your actual goal for our conversation?" Or "Son, I hope I'm wrong, but when you speak to me that way, it sounds as if you've started losing respect for me. Why don't you help me understand what's really behind your tone of voice?"

The key to this is that you must actually hope you're wrong. If you don't, choose another strategy.

What Do I Know About the Other Person?

Lesson 1

Who's on First?

*Now when the queen of Sheba heard of the fame
of Solomon concerning the name of the LORD, she
came to test him with hard questions. (1 Kings 10:1)*

Our next step is to move from focusing on what (as in what we want) to contemplating an important "who." Who is this other person (or people) with whom we plan to talk, and what do we know about them?

Reading didn't come easily to my dyslexic son, but he has a bright and active mind. From early childhood, Zack's bedtime routine involved listening to books on tape. He has a keen funny bone, so he was thrilled when we discovered a set of recorded shows from the Golden Age of Radio. Zack particularly loved the old Abbott and Costello bit called "Who's on First?" an amusingly confusing play on pronouns and names. He'd roar with laughter. When visitors came, he'd greet them with the line, "Who's on first?" and then fall to the floor giggling as if he'd invented comedy.

My son's funny bone was key to our communication through his teen years (and still is today). When we had hard topics to discuss, I knew if I could find a way to do it with humor, he'd be more willing to dialogue.

One method I used was a cartoon strip called *Zits*, featuring teen-age Jeremy Duncan. Many of the panels are a commentary on Jeremy's relationship with his parents, Walt and Connie. All characters, teen to adult, have assets and foibles, making them relatable for multiple generations, so I purchased several book-length collections.

I'd read several pages, bookmark them with a note saying, "This is you," and leave it in my son's room. I'd hear Zack chuckle as he read them. They might be about Jeremy not cleaning his room or spending hours sleeping instead of enjoying a beautiful Saturday.

Shortly after, he'd return the book with a new bookmark and note, "This is you." I'd find pages marked where Jeremy's mom said something embarrassing in front of a girl or overreacted to one of Jeremy's misadventures. We covered a lot of hard conversational territory through those comics.

What we know about the people with whom we intend to speak will inform our approach, tone, wording, and other aspects of our chat.

Consider what we know about their strengths, sensitivities, relationship with Jesus, opinion of the Bible, maturity, and culture. What's happening in their lives? Are they undergoing unusual stress? Are they in transition? If they're children or adolescents, what do we know about their stage of development? If they're seniors, do we understand what they can handle right now emotionally, mentally, or physically?

What do we already know about their opinions on the topic? How well do they know and trust us? Be careful to consider only what we know (because the person has told us) rather than what we think we know (because we've guessed or because we've heard from a third party).

Information is instrumental for an insightful approach to a hard conversation.

This sounds overwhelming, but it doesn't have to be. I'm not suggesting we compile a dossier on every person with whom we're about to talk, but too many conversations flounder or flare because we haven't given these details any consideration. Information is instrumental for an insightful approach to a hard conversation.

For instance, if we must tell our children we're moving to another state, we may not want to do it on the night before the SATs. If we're confronting the senior women's Bible study on their gossip habit, perhaps a football analogy isn't the best choice (unless they're NFL fans). Are we talking with an inner-city youth trying to get out of a gang? Maybe we avoid farming illustrations. Would knowing something about his or her sports/music/movie heroes give us a useful metaphor?

Could our conversation cause the other person discomfort or make that person emotional? Let's be sure we find a private location, not the back of the church after Sunday service. Does the other person have a tight schedule? Let's ask the person to set aside time to chat with us, not try to catch up in between appointments.

Are there physical or logistical impediments to consider? My dad has trouble hearing and doesn't always use his hearing aids. If I want to have a serious conversation with him, I don't do it over the telephone or in a busy location. I ensure I have his attention, that he's looking at me, and he's not distracted.

With some people, though, conversation will flow better if we're working side by side or playing a game of table tennis. This reduces the intensity of the situation and helps the other relax so the person can process what we're saying. Front porch rocking chairs or sitting on a wall by the ocean can both be conducive to healthy dialogue.

If we realize we're lacking knowledge about the people we're dealing with or understanding of their stage of life or current situation, we can make time to get to know them better. We can research stages of development or stresses on older adults. We can speak with people who know them better. It's a worthwhile investment of time.

ARTwork

Answer: Have you ever been confronted by someone who didn't know you well? What was the outcome of that experience?

Read: In 1 Kings 10:1–14, read about this powerful exchange between the Queen of Sheba and King Solomon. How do you suppose it affected the outcome of the queen's visit that she invested considerable time questioning Solomon about himself and his God?

Try: Get to know others better. Choose three people close to you and try to get to know them even better this week. Ask them, "What are some things I don't know or haven't noticed about you that are important for me to learn?" or "Tell me more about your interest in *X*" (as in a hobby, a worldview, or a life goal).

<hr>

Lesson 2

People We Know Well

When they got out on land, they saw a charcoal fire in place, with fish laid out on it, and bread. (John 21:9)

We don't always know what we think we know.

Depth of relationships can be measured on a spectrum from strangers to loved ones in our most intimate circle. Even within relationships, how well we know someone can fluctuate over time. Often, we even think we know someone better than we do. Let's talk about how depth of knowledge can impact conversation with people we know well, acquaintances, and strangers.

First, there are people we know well. This should be an advantage in a hard conversation, but don't be fooled. It's common to ignore, dismiss, or forget to account for what we know about someone close to us when considering a tough talk.

We can sometimes lose sight of people in our most intimate circles because they're such a part of the fabric of our days. Plus, ingrained habits of poor communication can complicate an already challenging topic. It's important to stop and reflect.

My twentysomething son was making choices I didn't like. He was coming to spend Easter with us, and these decisions weren't something I would ignore, but we were navigating new territory, feeling our way into a relationship of parent to adult child (emphasis on adult).

I prayerfully considered the framework for our conversation. I thought of my love for him and all the choices he'd made that were in line with the truth. He valued family and worked hard, so I thanked God for that. I recalled how stressed he was trying to navigate young adulthood and considered that he might be as frustrated with his life as we were. I also acknowledged I didn't know as much about him now as I did when he was a boy.

I reminded myself that in the past, I'd hurt him by flooding him with words. He wasn't one to react quickly, so I'd lecture him, trying to provoke a reaction until suddenly, he'd dissolve with the pain and the weight of my words. That was never productive, and I wanted to avoid doing it now. He's a sensitive guy and responds best with thoughtful information presented in a low-key way.

After lunch, he and I sat on the porch enjoying the hint of spring air. Following some silence, I spoke. "So, you're making some questionable decisions. I know I've taught you right from wrong. Why don't you tell me what you think I'm going to say?"

He laughed. Then he stated exactly what I'd been thinking. I didn't have to add a word. He covered it completely.

When he finished, I said, "Well, there. I couldn't have said it better. Help me, then, to understand your choices."

He explained his reasoning, and we had a productive discussion where he did most of the talking. It didn't change my mind on the rightness of his choices, but I had a better understanding of the pressures, thinking, and dynamics that factored into them. This set the stage for future conversations. Rather than hammer him with ultimatums or threaten the loss of our relationship, I stated biblical truth, set boundaries, and yet, created an open door for continued dialogue.

Did I receive my desired outcome? No. I would have preferred he immediately alter his choices. Didn't happen. He's an adult with his own relationship with Jesus. There's work going on between him and the Lord that isn't mine to meddle into once I've reminded him of the truth. But the conversation cleared the air between us and enabled us to move forward with integrity (and assured me he remembers what he learned from us growing up).

We prepare to speak with those we know well by recalling what we value about them, remembering their strengths, and considering their fears. We also review our understanding of how they best hear information. For example, is our father more likely to be receptive to hearing the gospel over coffee one-on-one, or does working alongside him in the garden lend itself to easier chats?

Are our children near enough in age and temperament that we can share news of our cancer with them together, or would individual conversations be more conducive to supporting them emotionally? What fears will arise and how can we be ready to address them?

What do we know about our newly separated friend's background and beliefs? Have others from our congregation already explained what they feel is sin? What has she not heard from others yet?

Is our daughter under pressure? When was the last time we affirmed her in what we see her doing well?

Does our spouse like a heads-up about a potentially intense conversation? Is our spouse more receptive to deep conversation in the morning with coffee or in the evening after dinner?

With every exchange, we can choose to extend or exhaust the bridge connecting us.

In close relationships, every hard conversation either fortifies the bridge between us or weakens it, so every subsequent hard conversation puts it at risk of collapse. With every exchange, we can choose to extend or exhaust the bridge connecting us.

Close relationships are worthy of the investment it takes to prepare properly. If a subject comes up before we've had time to prepare, there's wisdom in suggesting that we delay until a more opportune time (then immediately schedule that time so it doesn't become a perpetual postponement). Don't take those closest to us for granted. When approaching hard conversations with loved ones, it benefits everyone to prepare well.

ARTwork

Answer: What would those closest to you say are two of your strengths and one of your fears? How might that knowledge help them in having a hard conversation with you?

Read: After His resurrection, Jesus had to have a hard conversation with Peter, who'd denied Him three times. I love that Jesus came to Peter in his comfort zone, on the beach where he was fishing. Jesus provided a successful haul of fish, cooked for him, and then opened the conversation, one that clearly wasn't an easy one for Peter. Read John 21:1–19 and write what you can take from this as a model for your hard conversations.

Try: "Tell me what you imagine I'm going to say." This one line is a beautiful one to use with people close to us. It can be a shortcut through a lot of unnecessary words. One of the biggest mistakes I see families make is using too many words with one another that simply get tuned out—parent to child or spouse to spouse.

Rather than waste the airspace, in tense conversations, open with this wonderful line and experience the freedom it can bring. Either the other person captures your thoughts perfectly and spares you the drudgery of saying it, or that person is imagining worse than what you had planned to say, and your actual words will be a relief.

Lesson 3

People We Think We Know

> *When Moses' father-in-law saw all that he was*
> *doing for the people, he said, "What is this*
> *that you are doing for the people? Why do you*
> *sit alone, and all the people stand around you*
> *from morning till evening?" (Exod. 18:14)*

The second group to consider consists of our acquaintances. The trickiest people to plan for are those with whom we interact frequently but perhaps don't know as well as we think. Or maybe we know one aspect of their lives, but not others.

When my daughter was three, she stood at the door while I paid the pizza deliveryman. As he left, she shouted, "I love you, pizza man!"

Her burst of affection gave me pause, and I asked her, "Honey, why did you tell the pizza man you love him?"

"He's our friend, isn't he?" she replied. "We love our friends."

This inspired me to institute a new game called, "Is this a friend or a stranger we see often?" It's amazing the number of people, from the server at the coffee shop to the gas station attendant, who fall into the latter category (but whom my young children would have considered friends pregame).

I knew Hannah was catching on when she called out the car window to the gas attendant, "Hi, gas man. You're nice, but I wouldn't go anywhere with you unless Mom says we're friends. And right now, I can't love you because you're a stranger I just see often." (Parenting is a perpetual process of teaching, then fine-tuning.)

When considering hard conversations with acquaintances such as coworkers, church friends, or neighbors, we do well to take stock of what we know about them (not just what we think we know). We may know them well enough to have formed opinions about their lives, but not well enough to have the whole picture.

A friend (a self-identified turtle) told me about a woman who started attending her New England church. The woman stood out from the regulars because her clothes were flashy, form-fitting, and sometimes a little low-cut.

There was chatter behind the newcomer's back about her possible intentions and about the potential of her being a source of distraction from worship. Wisely, my friend nipped the gossip (and calmed the hawks) by offering to get to know her before anyone confronted her on making a wardrobe change (or accused her of worse).

 Learning more about a person can caution a hawk and embolden a turtle.

As it turned out, the woman had just moved from Central America. She had a pure heart for Jesus, and her clothing simply reflected her heritage. Without completely changing her flair, she eventually adapted to her more understated, adopted community (and they to her), and my friend became an intrepid advocate for the others to know and love her too. Learning more about a person can caution a hawk and embolden a turtle.

With acquaintances, if we can name two of their strengths, one of their fears, and articulate something of their family situation and interests outside the context in which we know them, that's a solid start. If not, maybe we need to know them better before initiating a hard conversation.

Sometimes when God prompts us to have these conversations, He doesn't intend us to have them immediately. If God prompted one of us to become a surgeon, we wouldn't expect to immediately set up shop with a scalpel in the backyard. We would anticipate needing to prepare before cutting into people. Poking around inside a person's life surely merits adequate time and preparation.

I'm not suggesting that knowing someone better should lead us to soften biblical truth or cause us to back down from saying hard things. Not at all. But even one-time hard conversations are a type of investment in another human being.

 Acquaintances are the stars of their own lives, not just supporting cast in ours.

The more we know about the other participant in our anticipated hard conversation, the more likely we are to set up the best situation for success. If we're not willing to learn more, that's a good indication that we need to check our impulse to speak out. People are creations of the almighty God, made in His image, not projects or statistics for our testimonies.

Depending on the setting, it may not be appropriate to delve deeply into other areas of that person's life. Remember there's always more going on than just the role we see played in our world. This reminder can reframe the conversation in our mind and inspire a humbler approach. Acquaintances are the stars of their own lives, not just supporting cast in ours.

For instance, we probably have some knowledge of our pastor, but when was the last time we considered his strengths, asked about his latest ministry challenges, or inquired (with compassion) about what makes him tick? Or our coworker. We know he likes to antagonize us with un-Christian remarks, but what else do we know about him? Does he have a family? Enjoy his work? What are his strengths? His fears? And Aunt Tilly. Do we know much about her beyond how much her laugh annoys us at family gatherings? What did she dream of being when she was younger? What does she read? Does she have hobbies or hopes?

We don't always get it right when we react to people without knowing them better.

ARTwork

Answer: What do you wish that coworkers or people in your church knew about you?

Read: Read Exodus 18:13–27. Observe how Jethro opens his conversation with Moses and the outcome.

Try: Tomorrow, choose two conversations to prayerfully consider at day's end. Ask God to help you devise an open-ended question that may have led to you learning more about the other person or helped move the conversation in a different direction.

Lesson 4

Strangers

*And he made from one man every nation of mankind
to live on all the face of the earth, having determined
allotted periods and the boundaries of their dwelling
place, that they should seek God, and perhaps feel
their way toward him and find him. Yet he is actually
not far from each one of us. (Acts 17:26–27)*

This, of course, leaves us with our third group—total strangers. Sometimes we feel compelled to have hard conversations with people about whom we know almost nothing—perhaps because of a serendipitous meeting, a connection on social media, or contact at a public gathering. It can be done, and there are occasions where it's appropriate, but it's still wise to assess what we do know.

In the eighties, I spent a summer on a mission trip to a rural region of Japan. I knew enough Japanese to get by, but that's not saying much. Most of the lovely people in that small city were eager for opportunities to practice their English, but it's not always necessary to understand a stranger's language to get the message.

One hot August morning, I was shopping at the local grocery store when an elderly gentleman started pointing at me and shouting. I wasn't aware of any cultural offense, but he was clearly angry. A crowd gathered. Bystanders glanced at me sideways. I considered using what Japanese I knew to ask the gentleman what I had done wrong, but before I spoke, I asked myself what I could know about him before I started speaking.

Suddenly, I realized his age meant he had likely experienced World War II, and this was the anniversary of the day Japan surrendered. It became clear to me that my American face was not a happy reminder. I dropped my gaze and bowed low before him in respect. A kind gentleman from the church then helped me exit quickly from the market so I would no longer be a reminder of a difficult historic period.

Another time, however, I arrived to speak at a weekend event only to realize with dismay that the couple charged with organizing—hadn't. With only hours before others arrived, we had to pull together a program with activities based on the event's theme. Initially I was concerned about their commitment to their group. Thank God He nudged me to ask more about them before I launched into a lecture about organization.

"Things are clearly not as ready as you'd intended them to be. Tell me about yourselves." They had recently responded to God's call on their lives to go out on a limb and serve a refugee population in their area. The work had blossomed more quickly than they'd imagined it would, and they weren't accustomed to delegating. They were on fire for Christ but embarrassed that timing had gotten away from them.

Rather than talk about organization, we had a frank conversation about setting limits, asking for help, and engaging teams. We not only outlined the weekend, but we also worked out a plan for them to establish a team for their next event at the end of this one. We'd sat down as strangers but rose as coworkers for Christ.

If a hard conversation arises with strangers or people we know very little, we don't simply abandon it, but instead, we ask ourselves what can be observed in the moment. Are we familiar with their culture? Generational context? Can we see an immediate and apparent stressor such as a crying child, a long line, or a public disaster?

> **If we don't know someone well, we should strive to know them well enough to have our facts straight.**

We don't always have to know people well before engaging in hard conversations, but if we don't know someone well, we should strive to know them well enough to have our facts straight. We can even engage in more effective hard conversations with strangers if we're willing to ask just one or two questions before we launch into our responses using the approach we've discussed in previous lessons.

Of course, it's not possible (or profitable) to know everyone in our conversations in depth, but asking the question—What do I know about the other person?—reminds us there are more people in the dialogue than just us. Hawks are too often simply invested in making sure their thoughts are heard, while turtles can be so focused on their own discomfort, they forget another person may need to hear what they have to say. This "other" focus can pull us both back into effective conversational attitudes.

In cases where it can't be avoided, lack of knowledge about the other can be managed by simply acknowledging that truth. In your own words, say something like, "I'm happy to discuss this with you, but we don't know each other very well. I want to have a respectful discussion, so please interrupt me if I offend or you feel there may be something that is important for me to know."

Then, proceed with confidence in Christ but caution regarding your own humanity. Pay attention to the other person's body language. Check in frequently. Ask clarifying questions to be sure you understand what's being said or asked before you respond.

What we know about people and what we value about them can inform our approach, tone, depth of content, and logistics of our conversation.

ARTwork

Answer: What do you know about that person with whom you want to talk? Name two strengths, one fear, something about that person's family situation, and one interest.

Read: Paul was in a strange city, but he observed the people and culture long enough to gain an appreciation for their interests and to notice their idols. Read Acts 17:16–32, then look around a setting where you'd like to share the gospel. Ask God to open your eyes to the possibilities you haven't been seeing.

Try: Choose five people to get to know better this week (include one stranger). Choose a question. Then ask one person a day for five days. What did you learn? How did others react to your question? Did anything surprise you? Sample questions: What was your favorite story, movie, or television show growing up? Are you doing what you dreamed you would be doing at your age, and if not, what was your dream? Who had the most influence on you as a teenager and why? Where do you fall in the line of your siblings and how do you think that shaped your personality?

Lesson 5

Using, Not Abusing, What We Know

And the LORD sent Nathan to David. He came to him and said to him, "There were two men in a certain city, the one rich and the other poor." (2 Sam. 12:1)

In 2 Samuel 12, the prophet Nathan had the unenviable job of having a hard conversation with the king. David committed adultery with

Bathsheba, and orchestrated the death of her husband, Uriah. God tasked Nathan with confronting David on his sin.

It's no coincidence that Nathan chose to tell David a story about two men and one little sheep. His story elements brought David right back to his youth as a shepherd, a time when David's heart was completely yielded to God and he had been diligent about protecting his flock. God used Nathan's brilliantly conceived story to bring David to repentance.

One of my ministry partners asked me to consult with a man she was counseling. He was at risk of losing his wife because he refused to discipline their children. They'd tried many techniques, but nothing was working for him.

I first asked him to tell me about himself—his parents, his upbringing, and what he did for work. I learned his father had been a hard man and quick to use corporal punishment. This was the man's only reference for a father disciplining his child. For work, he was leader of a team of first responders called in for hazardous material emergencies.

"Do the people who work for you respect you and do what you say?" I asked.

"Of course. We're a very tight team. I'm proud to say we have very little turnover."

"Are you ever afraid you're being too hard on them or that they won't like you?"

He shrugged. "I am hard on them sometimes, but they know it's my job and that it makes us a stronger team. I don't worry whether or not they like me because I'm doing the right thing."

"Do they like you?"

He didn't hesitate. "Yeah, they like me. Hey, I think I know where you're going with this. Are you saying I can use some of my work skills with my family? I mean, is that all right? Could it work?" (I wasn't saying anything, but often the right questions help people reach the best conclusions.)

My ministry partner brightened. "It's certainly worth exploring. Let's discuss techniques you use with your team and see what transfers best to parenting."

Often, mining the context of a person's life provides wonderful language to use during hard conversations. In Acts 17, Paul observed the culture of Athens. He was disturbed by their idols but also made two key observations. One, the Athenians and foreigners spent their days telling and hearing new things; and two, they had an idol dedicated to "the unknown god." When he spoke to them, he referenced the "new way" created by Christ and used the idol to an unknown god as a launchpad for introducing the God of the universe. Brilliant.

Jesus had the advantage of knowing us better than we know ourselves, but observe how he interacts with people. With the woman at the well, He referenced water. When He called His first disciples—fishermen—He offered to make them fishers of men. When speaking with the people of Israel, He referenced bread, wineskins, sowing seeds, and oil lamps. All everyday items or actions with which they were familiar.

> **Just as any carpenter's tool can be turned into a weapon, so relational and conversational skills can be used by unscrupulous people to manipulate rather than communicate.**

The better we know the other person—and leverage that knowledge— the more hope we have of effective communication. This doesn't mean we access our understanding of the other person for the purpose of manipulation. Just as any carpenter's tool can be turned into a weapon, so relational and conversational skills can be used by unscrupulous people to manipulate rather than communicate. Don't be that person.

Jesus followers rely on the Holy Spirit to move a person to change, not on emotional trickery. The key to Nathan's storytelling session with King David is found in verse 1 of 2 Samuel 12: "And the LORD sent Nathan to David." *God* initiated the confrontation and worked through Nathan. Like Nathan, we consider what we know about others from a desire to please God and serve others.

ARTWORK

Answer: What stories, metaphors, or reference points resonate with you?

Read: Nathan's story is found in 2 Samuel 11–12:25. Notice Nathan also brings word of God's love for David following his repentance. We not only confront with truth, but we also encourage with truth.

Try: Practice storytelling. One vehicle for hard conversations is story. Stories come in books or as sermon illustrations, but we also hear stories in songs, watch them on screens, or listen to them on the radio. It works well with children and teens if you can find a book, song, or movie (one that's age appropriate) to share and use as an introduction to a hard topic. When we observe someone else tackling a hard subject, it provides reference points for us to discuss it.

HEART OF THE ART PRACTICE

Sit One Out

Talking over others can become a habit, especially for hawks. Next time you're with a group, one in which you're usually an active voice, set your watch for ten minutes and "sit out" the conversation. Absorb the conversations around you. Tune in to the topics others choose. Pay attention to their style and pace of speaking. Note how often the conversation volleys from one person to another. Remind yourself of the beauty and joy of listening. (This is also a wonderful assignment to give to the person who talks too often in your small group. Tell that person you'd like assistance noticing who talks and who stays quiet. Ask the person to spend a week listening and recording who needs to be encouraged to speak more often.)

Do the Next Thing

Turtles become easily overwhelmed talking with others about problems they're experiencing or changes they need to make. Often, it's because we think we need to get everyone to the final goal in one conversation. This rarely happens.

It can be helpful to keep in mind that all anyone can actually do is to take the next step, to do the next thing. Turtles excel with this kind of approach. When you're reaching the end of a conversation, it can be especially helpful to ask, "What do you see as a next step you can take . . ." (to address your spiritual growth, or to give up that habit, or to move through grief)? "What's the next thing you can do . . ." (to achieve your goal, or to make amends with that person, or to discover more about Jesus)?

What Emotions May Be Involved in This Conversation?

Lesson 1

Taking a Cue from Jesus

"And you shall love the Lord your God with all your heart and with all your soul and with all your mind and with all your strength." The second is this: "You shall love your neighbor as yourself." There is no other commandment greater than these.
(Mark 12:30–31)

The first time a spiritual leader accused me of being emotional, I was a teenager, so in his defense, it wasn't a huge leap. Distraught, I arrived in his office with questions of a theological nature. There I was, a weeping middle schooler, initiating a hard conversation.

What moved me to tears? It was Easter week. Our pastor, the same man whose office I entered sobbing, had exhorted us from the pulpit to meditate on what Jesus endured in the days leading up to the cross. So, I had.

I thought about His betrayal, arrest, and abandonment by His friends. I meditated on the rigged trials, humiliation, beatings, and rejection by His own people. Images flooded my thoughts of Jesus flogged, the walk to Calvary, and the crucifixion. This was the Jesus I loved, and so, as I considered all He'd endured to pay the price for my sins, it moved me.

Something else opened within me that week too. For the first time, I was flooded with an impassioned concern for all souls living and dead. I came to this pastor with questions about the unreached and the future of souls who lived before the cross.

Eventually, I learned satisfying answers to those questions, but it wasn't on that day. After I managed to voice my concerns between sobs, the only response he offered was a hand wave and these words: "Lori, come back when you aren't so emotional."

I'd certainly been charged with that before, but this was the first time it came from a spiritual leader. It confused me—especially since my repellant state developed following his instructions. What had he expected would happen from a week of meditating on Jesus's suffering? I was crying, but it was my mind that sought answers. I hadn't come asking for tissues and hugs.

That experience kept me from asking him any other questions unless I was certain I could do it without expressing any kind of emotion. While I'm sure that made his life more comfortable, he missed on an opportunity to guide a young Christian through the maze of feelings evoked by a proper understanding of Christ's sacrifice and the condition of those who don't follow Him.

Instead, I muddled around for a couple more decades with this vague notion that "emotional" Christians weren't quite welcome in the thinking church. This was reinforced by other Christians who considered all expressions of emotions suspect. The mind, it seemed to them, unlike emotions, was perfectly reliable and redeemable, but the heart was doomed. With that misunderstanding, I set about to develop my mind and ignore my emotions, in what I thought was Jesus's plan for me. Instead, it was a path destructive to my spirit and my relationships.

Feelings aren't failings. They're gifts from our generous God.

I was relieved when Jesus set me straight—which He did with the advantage of spiritual maturity and His Word. I now understand feelings aren't failings. They're gifts from our generous God who desires us to experience Him with our whole being—heart, mind, soul, and strength.

We shouldn't be ruled by emotions, and we certainly aren't to let emotions dictate our theology, but it's misguided to believe that somehow Jesus would redeem our souls and minds but leave feelings out of His purview. As if some deficiency in His design makes emotions such a danger that even when following Jesus, they must be forever suspect.

Having a biblically informed view of God's design for feelings can go a long way to free us to engage in tense discussions. Hard conversations are rife with emotions. Fear of facing emotions is a powerful incentive to avoid them. Expending energy trying to squelch or manage emotions during hard conversations is often an unproductive waste of resources.

To imagine we'll engage in these talks and be able to contain or divorce our feelings from the equation is ludicrous. And why would we? Emotions are a gift from God. He designed them, and despite the challenges they present, they serve a purpose, not the least of which is to reflect Him.

Jesus was fully human. He both experienced and expressed a wide range of emotions. He wept (John 11:35), loved (John 19:26), and conveyed compassion (Matt. 9:36), joy (Luke 10:21), and anger (Mark 3:1–6). Isaiah prophesied that "He was despised and rejected by men, a man of sorrows and acquainted with grief" (Isa. 53:3).

While He gave expression to His emotions, we don't see Him ruled by them, but by obedience to the Father: "If you keep my commandments, you will abide in my love, just as I have kept my Father's commandments and abide in his love" (John 15:10).

> **While emotions shouldn't be stuffed or ignored, the final word on them is the Lord's.**

Like a lot of studious, chubby kids, I wasn't popular in school. Sometimes I'd sulk about it. My mom would say, "People may love you, they may hate you. Either way, it doesn't make you any taller or shorter, Lori Ann. Their feelings don't decide who you are."

It bugged me when she said it, but it was true. Jesus didn't rise or fall with the emotions of others toward Him. In the week leading to the crucifixion, the crowd initially exalted Him. Days later, they demanded His death. Still, He was secure in His Father whether the people clamored for a king or called for a cross. Jesus demonstrated daily that while emotions shouldn't be stuffed or ignored, the final word on them is the Lord's.

Christians sometimes think God is like the aliens from an old episode of *Star Trek*—just giant brains considering great thoughts but entertaining no feelings. In Jesus, we encounter a thinking-feeling person, acknowledging but not ruled by either his mind or his emotions, but by His Father. In Christ, "all things hold together" (Col. 1:17), including our emotions.

Being disciples of the Creator of emotions should put us in a prime position to be leaders in the world when it comes to both managing and expressing them. This isn't exactly the church's history, but that doesn't mean it's out of reach.

ARTwork

Answer: What messages about emotions did you receive from your family, church, and community growing up? What are your thoughts about those messages now?

Read: Psalm 22 is rife with powerful emotions and is prophetic of Jesus's last hours on the cross. As you read, note the range of feelings expressed. Then read Mark 14:32–42, Jesus praying in Gethsemane. Note the emotions Jesus expresses to His Father in prayer.

Try: Become unguarded before God. When preparing for hard conversations, we sometimes try to fix ourselves before we pray and come to God praying like this: "Lord, I just want whatever You want from this conversation. May Your will be done." Which is a fine prayer unless what you believe in your heart is that you're right, the other person is wrong, and you hope that God's will is for the other person to see the light and change. Jesus was unguarded before His Father in prayer as was David, a man after God's own heart.

Read the Psalms, and you'll find the start of many of David's psalms sound closer to our inner reality than to the fine sounding prayers we think will impress Him. By the end, though, God worked on David's heart, because David came to Him unguarded. If we show up, unguarded, before God, He'll uncover our hidden attitudes and address them before we open our mouths to others.

Wholly Fallen, Wholly Redeemed

And I will give you a new heart, and a new spirit I will put within you. And I will remove the heart of stone from your flesh and give you a heart of flesh. (Ezek. 36:26)

While our emotions are created by God to have a beautiful purpose, they are, like the rest of who we are, fallen.

There are certainly times our emotions are unreliable. Feelings can be impacted by a variety of factors including physical (fatigue, hormones, brain chemistry), spiritual (sin, deceptions, strongholds), situational (stress, grief, abuse), mental (perceptions, capacity, and disorder), and cultural (ethnic norms, prevailing trends, familial traditions). However, there's no reason to maintain that just because on some occasions emotions can't be trusted, that they are beyond the work of Christ. The Bible is clear that God's plan for redemption includes our feelings as well.

Psalm 37:4 says, "Delight yourself in the LORD, and he will give you the desires of your heart." Why would He do that, if our hearts are endlessly corrupt? Meditating on this verse served as a wedge in the door I'd slammed on my emotional life.

God then directed me to other verses that enlightened me on the truth that His redemptive work includes the whole person. These included Jeremiah 24:7: "I will give them a heart to know that I am the LORD, and they shall be my people and I will be their God, for they shall return to me with their whole heart." And Ezekiel 36:26: "And I will give you a new heart, and a new spirit I will put within you. And I will remove the heart of stone from your flesh and give you a heart of flesh."

God supplies us with new hearts—and not cold stone (or titanium), but hearts of flesh that beat and bleed. This was a revelation to me, but one that made biblical sense. Imagine the disaster that would ensue if my husband restored our entire century-old house but left the ancient wiring untouched. No carpenter would be able to sleep at night with that kind of work undone, and neither does our Father God. He redeems the whole person and doesn't leave behind faulty feelings to risk a dangerous spark. The whole person is fallen; the whole person is redeemed.

And for the record, the mind isn't so exempt from the need for ongoing sanctification either. Romans 12:2 explains it can be polluted, and it too needs transformation. Our minds function with greater clarity when we acknowledge the biblical truth that thoughts can be as suspect as emotions if they aren't taken captive to Christ as Paul cautions us in 2 Corinthians 10:5.

All of God's design serves a purpose. Why would emotions be any different? Of course, they've been affected by sin, but what is their original intent?

Emotions are one manner by which we connect with God and with others. Feelings also serve as signs, like dashboard warning lights, when things are awry. They function as motivators to do what is right and avoid what is wrong.

> **Rather than trying to hide, deny, or dismiss emotions, we acknowledge, name, and discuss them with God.**

As we grow in a biblical understanding of the role feelings play in the lives of believers, we travel the path of truly governing them. Rather than trying to hide, deny, or dismiss emotions, we acknowledge, name, and discuss them with God. Our emotional lives then emerge from the darkness into His light, and work in conjunction with our minds rather than quietly sabotaging from the shadows.

Our minds, bodies, and emotions, in the process of redemption and sanctification, grow to function with truly remarkable integrity. As important as mental and spiritual preparation, emotional preparation is crucial to a productive hard conversation.

ARTwork

Answer: What are ways your emotions help you connect with God and with others? How are they a blessing in your life?

Read: Psalms 19:12–14 and 139:23–24. Is anything hidden from our God—even our deep feelings?

Try: Lower your shields. In battle, when facing a perceived threat, warriors raise their shields. This is appropriate in battle—not helpful in relationships. Anger has its place, but it can be an overused shield.

If you acknowledge anger toward the other person in your hard conversation, ask God to reveal what's behind the anger. Anger can be the armor that appears when we feel hurt, disappointed, threatened, unappreciated, disrespected, dishonored, worried, afraid, shocked, caught off guard, inconvenienced, or misunderstood.

Remember that God is your strength and shield—not anger. God makes a better protector than a feeling, even one as powerful as anger.

Then, express the underlying feeling in a God-honoring way. Instead of saying, "John, I'm so angry with you about that sermon," say, "John, I'm disappointed at the views you expressed in this sermon. I'm worried you're going off track biblically." Rather than saying, "Maggie, I've had it with you not calling when you're going to be late," say, "Maggie, when I sit here alone waiting long past the time we agreed to meet, I feel small, unimportant, and insignificant in your life." The angry expressions invite conflict. The alternate ones invite conversation.

Lesson 3

Hiding Is Not Helping

Can a man hide himself in secret places so that I cannot see him? declares the LORD. Do I not fill heaven and earth? declares the LORD. (Jer. 23:24) could see my two friends pulling away from each other. There hadn't been any disagreement of which I was aware. Both denied having any issues with the other, but the strain was clear. Finally, one late night at a retreat, after much prayer and conversation, one had the courage to speak.

"Okay, I'm jealous of you, Sharon. Crazy jealous. And you must know that. You're doing so much better than I am at reaching your goals, and you talk about it all the time."

Sharon responded, "You're jealous of me? How can you be? You have a husband and children, and I'm still single. I'm envious of you. I thought you were happy for me and my accomplishments. Whenever you talk about Tom and the kids, I talk more about those things just to keep up."

Months of relationship strain dissolved after a few moments of discomfort and honest confession. They named their feelings. Asked forgiveness of God and each other. Created a plan for better ways to share about their lives and granted permission to admit negative feelings in the future.

> **Since the fall of Adam and Eve, hiding has always been a temptation, but it's never a solution.**

The problem between my friends grew because they both tried to hide from their obvious feelings, rather than live in the light that freedom in Christ provides. Since the fall of Adam and Eve, hiding has always been a temptation, but it's never a solution. It creates a kind of false level of operating, and anything false is not in line with God's truth.

When you're preparing for a hard conversation, it's important to examine your feelings. What are your feelings toward the other person? Are you intimidated, afraid, envious, or ambivalent? Are you worried, nervous, or angry about that person? Do you feel superior, inferior, or equal? Is some small part of you happy the person merits correction?

Has the person hurt or disappointed you? Are you repelled or disgusted? Are you reminded of someone? Are you so enamored that you make allowances you shouldn't? Do you admire or respect that person?

Some feelings are understandable, and many are desirable. Others are unpleasant, unproductive, unbiblical, but still very present and real. This sorting process doesn't have to be rocket science, but it does take some courage and integrity.

First, come clean with God about your feelings. Name them. You may find you have feelings that conflict or contradict. We're human. That happens. Just list them all. (The Psalms provide a powerful, biblical example of this.) Don't try to dismiss the conflicts or contradictions at first. They can be informative.

Second, repent of any feelings that stem from sin, such as envy, hatred, or revenge. Ask God's forgiveness and seek a corrective, redemptive path. This path may include confessing these feelings to another person or resolving them with support from spiritual counsel. Using a concordance, look up Scriptures that address these feelings. It may help to reflect on these verses prior to your meeting.

Third, seek His guidance on when and how to share your feelings with the other person. If you decide to share difficult feelings with the other person, consider prayerfully the words you'll use to do so.

Our feelings must serve God, not our own agendas.

Own the emotions and invite the other person into a partnership with you around them. As in "I'm wrestling with my disappointment over your decision. I think it may help me if I have a better understanding of your reasoning. Would you be willing for us to discuss it?" or "I'm embarrassed to admit I'm jealous that you seem to be considering my sister's feelings in planning Mom's funeral, but you're not asking what I need. Before I take on more hurt, can we discuss this?"

Finally, prepare to reciprocate. What do you know of the other person's feelings toward you? Can you validate any of them? Are you prepared not to judge the feelings, but to trust God to help you sort through them together?

Strong emotions are drivers. We want the Holy Spirit to drive our hard conversations, so we need to bring every thought and emotion under His leadership and direction. We serve others by creating an atmosphere that facilitates them doing the same. Our feelings must serve God, not our own agendas.

In some ways, allowing people to honestly express emotions during a tough talk demonstrates a faith that God is bigger than those feelings and can still reign over what occurs. We can only control our own feelings (and barely that sometimes). Trying to manage, contain, or minimize someone else's emotions too often utilizes energy and conversational resources better used employing biblically informed skills.

ARTwork

Answer: What emotions are hard for you to manage or face? What are strategies you've found helpful for coping with strong feelings?

Read: In Luke 7:36–50, a woman expresses her intense love for Jesus by washing His feet with her hair before a room full of "important" people, including the Pharisee hosting the meal. Jesus doesn't condemn her outpouring and, in fact, uses her as an example for His hardened host. With whom do you identify in this story, and why?

Try: Work on ground rules. In hard conversations, it can be useful to establish a few ground rules. This is particularly useful with groups but can even benefit conversations involving only two people. It's only fair that everyone involved be invited to contribute to the ground rules. Simply open by acknowledging you're about to talk about a sensitive subject and believe it will be helpful to set some boundaries.

Sample ground rules follow.

"Let's agree to keep our voices calm and speak at a volume we'd use in a restaurant."

"If anyone needs a five-minute break, we'll pause."

"We're only going to talk about this incident. We're not going to discuss in this conversation anything that happened prior to today."

The key to having ground rules is enforcing them. One simple method is to explain the ground rules and then state that if someone violates one, you're going to hold up your hand as a reminder. Or empower everyone to enforce the rules by raising a hand when one of them is violated. Ask the group how they would suggest the ground rules be enforced. This method provides a shared responsibility that can build teamwork.

Lesson 4

Being Present with Emotional People

And standing behind him at his feet, weeping, she began to wet his feet with her tears and wiped them with the hair of her head and kissed his feet and anointed them with the ointment. (Luke 7:38)

A staff person rushed to my cubicle. "Can you help?" she asked. "There's an angry man here."

A tall man I didn't know, except by name, stood in the hallway. One of my partners usually worked with him. "Arthur, can I help you?" I asked.

He stepped into my personal space, shaking and shouting, "You'd better be able to help me! No one's answering my calls. I can't handle being ignored, you know. I sound angry, and I am, but that's my issue. Bad stuff happened to me when I was just a little guy, and I don't handle it well when it feels like people are abandoning me. You understand? Right now, I need someone to pay attention."

The staff person sneaked away.

He was so close, I could smell what he'd had for lunch, but I didn't back up. I kept my arms at my sides and stood very still. "So, you're not angry with me; you're angry because that happens when you feel abandoned. You need someone to listen right now to calm down. Is that right?"

He didn't reduce his volume but relaxed his position and took one step back. "Yes! That's it. Can you do that?"

I loved that he was able to articulate exactly what motivated his outburst. I wish everyone could be so clear.

When we express emotions, there can be many reasons why. Though triggered by an immediate situation, it's likely a host of other factors are affecting our choice of emotion, intensity, pattern of expression, and path to resolution. Like a spouting whale, with emotions there's generally much more creature lurking below the surface than just the obvious spray.

> **Like a spouting whale, with emotions there's generally much more creature lurking below the surface than just the obvious spray.**

Emotions are like the steam set off by our thoughts. If we stuff them for too long, whether as individuals or communities, at some point, the steam forces an escape and can be explosive. There's an argument to be made that for decades, the church clamped a lid on emotional expression and now it's blown. The biblical answer isn't to restrain or release emotion with abandon, but to harness or channel its power, so it's a boon and not a burn.

My friend returned depressed from a weekend with her in-laws. Her husband was sullen and withdrawn.

"What happened?" I asked.

She sighed. "My mother-in-law started therapy. Apparently, her therapist encouraged her to express herself."

I tilted my head to the side. "Okay, and . . ."

She threw up her hands. "She did. All weekend. Every angry, depressive, selfish, critical, vindictive thought she's had for the past twenty years spewed out on us all. 'You don't want me to lie, do you?' she kept repeating. My husband is destroyed. I never want to go back. How can this be a healthy way to live? And when anyone challenged her, she just said, 'My therapist says I have a right to express my feelings and to feel any way I feel.'"

> **Our rights become our wrongs when we toss them like darts at those we're called to love.**

James warns against this practice of spewing unpleasant feelings onto others in James 3:13–17. We have every right to acknowledge our feelings, and because God calls us to truthful lives, we shouldn't ever hide behind masks. However, we don't have the right to assault others with our expression of those feelings. Our rights become our wrongs when we toss them like darts at those we're called to love.

My friend and her husband didn't want his mother to bottle up those awful feelings. They were concerned for her and the pain she was experiencing. But simply expressing them without restraint wasn't the answer. Her therapist eventually agreed, inviting her family to have those conversations during a session rather than at random events. Then the feelings could be processed with guidance from someone skilled at sorting through trauma.

When people experience overpowering emotions that we feel ill-equipped to handle, an alternative to avoiding them or shutting them down is to include in the conversation a third party with counseling gifts or clinical skills. Extreme sadness, rage, chronic anxiety, frequent fear, severe mood swings, or feelings of worthlessness can be signs of more serious mental health concerns that can be identified and treated with professional support.

God doesn't hold us responsible for other people's feelings, and we shouldn't take that on. He does hold us accountable for our thoughts, words, and actions, as well as our own emotions. That's plenty for us to worry about.

In preparing for hard conversations, we don't need to plan how to interpret or analyze what's behind other people's feelings, but we should remind ourselves that their reaction is likely as much about them as it is about us.

We can increase the chance that emotions won't dominate, undermine, or be ignored in our hard conversations. Preparatory heart-work predisposes us to manage our own feelings. Our word choices, our tone of voice, and the setting for our conversations can all become tools to serve both parties and facilitate communication rather than escalation. Also, timing, as they say, is everything. It's crucial to consider the best timing for us and for the other person, especially when navigating chronic emotions.

Ken was a grumpy old man. Cranky as they come. Daily, he donned a scowl and a sour attitude and then brought it to the fitness center where I worked.

Everything bothered Ken. The equipment wasn't clean enough. The temperature was off. The weightlifters grunted too loud and slammed too hard. The whole place was mismanaged.

Understandably, no one wanted to go near him. Most of the staff avoided him until he cornered them to express his litany of concerns.

I wish I could say I had some brilliant plan that worked to bring Ken around, but my approach wasn't born of forethought, as much as from my desire to take my lumps when I was fresh and energized. I also knew I needed the element of surprise with Ken, not to ensnare him, but so I was best prepared to respond to him with grace. While others relied on avoidance to handle him, I'd read *The Art of War*. Prepare, don't ensnare, became my motto.

The moment I arrived on shift, I'd beeline for Ken. "Good morning, Mr. Howell. It's good to see you working out. I'm hoping you'll be willing to help me."

He'd squint his eyes and scowl. "Young lady, I'm not here to help you. You're here to assist me, and I've noticed that towel dispenser in the corner has been empty for thirty minutes."

I scribbled a note on my clipboard. "Wonderful. That's excellent information. It's precisely that type of feedback I know you'll provide. I understand from the staff that you have an eye for quality control. I take our goal to serve our customers seriously. If you don't mind, I'm going to check in with you daily. Let's see if, together, we can improve this place."

He glanced around as if to look for hidden cameras and then gave me a disgusted grimace. "Just get towels in that dispenser. Oh," he added as I turned away, "and the radio is too loud." I noted that.

I repeated this approach every day. At first he'd wave me off after noting his complaints, but in a couple of weeks, we moved on to other topics. I learned what he did before he retired. I asked about his family. He told me about his health challenges. We discussed the news, and as we chatted, I introduced him to other members exercising around him. He took a shine to one of our developmentally disabled adults, Doris, and helped her if she struggled with any of the machines.

After a month or so, as I approached, I heard him remark to another gentleman, "That's Lori. She and I practically run this place. My name's Ken. What's yours?" He offered his hand to the man with a smile. Three weeks later, he and his new friend serenaded Doris on her birthday, while she blushed and giggled on the recumbent bike.

> **Embracing conflict when you're prepared trumps encountering it when you're cornered.**

This story makes for a lovely anecdote, but let me tell you, those first few weeks were no picnic. His crankiness was deeply ingrained. I doubted my approach every day. It took a long time to build trust. My plan wasn't born out of courage, but as a survival strategy. Still, I learned that embracing conflict when you're prepared trumps encountering it when you're cornered.

I've repeated this strategy with numerous "problem" people and have always experienced a positive outcome after an investment of time (and ego).

ARTWORK

Answer: What are healthy ways you've found to let off emotional steam?

Read: In Lamentations 3, we're privy to Jeremiah processing heavy-duty emotions before God and emerging to a place of faith. He clearly doesn't hold back. At what verse do we see the prophet's turning point? How can this be a model for praying through our own strong feelings?

Try: Utilize the dentist's method. Most people dread going to the dentist, but I love going to mine. Even when I'm having work done, he makes it a soothing experience.

As soon as he enters the room, he greets me in a way that lets me know he sees me as a person and not just another patient. "Lori, it's good to see you again. How are your parents adjusting to your dad's retirement?"

He then identifies why I'm there. "It's my understanding that we're going to address that tooth that needs a crown today. Is that your understanding too?"

Then he walks me through what is about to take place.

Shortly after he begins work, he checks in. Is this progressing as I expected? Am I experiencing pain? If I need him to pause at any point, I just need to ask.

The dentist's method is a model we can access when facing challenging emotions in hard conversations. Whether we use this approach as only self-talk or with others, it can provide a framework for navigation through tough feelings.

HEART OF THE ART PRACTICE

Offering Options

Hawks often enter conversations with only one solution in mind. We're so clear on our point and comfortable with our perspective, we approach people with not just the problem but also a prescribed answer. People may agree with us about the problem, but if they reject our solution, we become stuck and feel the conversation was fruitless. It helps to come into discussions with several possible choices the other person could make.

For instance, if we're having a hard conversation about choosing to follow Jesus, of course, we'd love if the person prayed right then. However, if the person senses this is the only option that will make us happy, that individual may avoid future conversations. No one wants to be a continual disappointment.

Instead, perhaps we offer several options such as "If you'd like to know more about what I've said, I'd be happy to talk again. Or maybe we can just keep being friends and enjoying football games together. Of course, if you ever do decide to follow Jesus, I'm here to support you in any way I can."

If the other person is a loved one with whom you've had to share news of your illness, that individual may not be able to discuss it in the moment. It may be overwhelming. We can offer this loved one a range of options that might sound like this: "I'm happy for us to discuss your feelings about this news right now, but I've had longer to absorb it than you have. We can keep talking now, or we can resume our chat after dinner. Or you're welcome to talk with Pastor Todd or Aunt Glenda. They're safe people who care about us."

In a conflict situation, it may sound like this: "The elders want you to step down as chairperson for a variety of reasons. You and I can discuss this privately, we can entertain a conversation with the entire board, or you can take a few days to consider another path for us to take. What feels most comfortable right now?"

The pastor who told me to come back when I was not so emotional could have offered me a better option. He might have validated that it's appropriate to feel powerful sadness at the crucifixion of our Lord and it made sense that I was overwhelmed. He might then have suggested that since I was asking such important and complex questions, perhaps he could address one that afternoon and schedule another time to discuss the others. Perhaps when I'd had more time to process my feelings.

A range of options empowers the other person and keeps us in check, so we don't overwhelm that person or shut down conversation by limiting solutions to the ones we can see prior to our conversation.

Panic Prevention Phrase

Many turtles experience initial panic at the idea of having to supply an immediate answer. The good news is that others usually don't need answers as immediately as we think they do.

One strategy for managing this panic is to employ one simple phrase, "Before I answer . . ."

As in "Before I answer, I'd like to make sure I understand exactly what you're asking."

Or "Before I answer, may I ask what sparked your interest in this subject?"

Or "Before I answer, what do you know about Jesus?" Or whatever else the question has been about.

This only works if you employ it as something other than a delay tactic. You must say the phrase and then truly listen to the answer, as opposed to using that talk time to formulate your response.

After you have listened, often God will provide you with the right words, which may be another question, and another. We aren't God-answer machines, like slots. We're simply people who know God, sitting with others God loves and wants to reach—through us.

Be a person. Get real. Understand what you're being asked, and who's asking, by seeking information before you answer.

What Biblical Guidelines Exist for This Conversation? (Is It Based in Truth?)

Lesson 1

Tongue Control

Set up road markers for yourself;
make yourself guideposts;
consider well the highway,
the road by which you went.
(Jer. 31:21)

The guardrails we install along our roads and highways are neither attractive nor inspiring, but that's not their purpose. There's nothing more serious than a guardrail, and that's because they exist for the grave function of minimizing the danger of accidents and falls. I experienced the brutal protection of a guardrail myself one wintry morning.

As my husband and I traveled a dark, snowy road to drop him at his job site, we skidded on an icy, unplowed patch of highway and found ourselves spinning across both lanes. We were headed for a deep ditch bordering a line of solid trees until our car made violent contact with the galvanized steel that saved our lives.

The force of the collision combined with the jarring restraint of my seat belt left me with a painful chest injury that would take weeks to heal. Our car suffered front-end damage. Still, it's a certainty that we would have incurred much greater wounds, possibly fatal, and more extensive destruction to our vehicle without the existence of that barrier. You might say the lesser wound was a kindness served by the authority that installed the guardrail.

Biblical guidelines are intended to be corrective, but also protective.

While it's no fun to discuss guidelines and biblical rules for speech, they serve as conversational guardrails that exist for our good and protection, installed by the highest authority who works all things together for good for those who love Him (Rom. 8:28). Reminding one another of these principles and working to obey them may be painful at times, but that is a lesser wound than the damage caused when people operate tongues without consideration for the power they wield. Biblical guidelines are intended to be corrective, but also protective.

James has much to say about the tongue. James 1:26 should be a strong caution to us: "If anyone thinks he is religious and does not bridle his tongue but deceives his heart, this person's religion is worthless." He goes on to explain what a monumental task it is to bridle the tongue when he says, "For every kind of beast and bird, of reptile and sea creature, can be tamed and has been tamed by mankind, but no human being can tame the tongue. It is a restless evil, full of deadly poison" (James 3:7–8). I stop and catch my breath every time I read that passage, it's so strong in its warning.

When we read James's words, we can be tempted to believe there's no hope for managing our speech in biblical ways, but what is impossible for humans is possible with God (Matt. 19:26). It's the "with God" part that we often neglect when it comes to speaking.

Learning to safely drive a two-ton vehicle down a highway at sixty-five miles per hour is a task best done with someone already skilled in the task. My husband has greater faith than I do, so he did most of the driving instruction for our two children.

On the occasions when I was the only one available, I took them to the local cemetery that had miles of winding road but reduced opportunity for causing harm to the living. They had learned the rules of the road, passed tests for learning permits, and had the motivation, but they still needed to be with a veteran driver to learn. Similarly, we need God next to us when we're learning our way around conversations that matter.

 ## We need God next to us when we're learning our way around conversations that matter.

Christians operate under the rule of God's Word. For every conversation, there are both global guidelines for us to keep in mind (or in mouth, as it were) as well as guidelines specific to our situation. And so, we benefit from asking, "What biblical guidelines exist for this conversation?"

First, keep overarching truths about speech in mind. Obviously, the fruit of the spirit—love, joy, peace, patience, kindness, goodness, faithfulness, gentleness, and self-control—should be evident, not only in our character and actions, but also in our words.

Paul tells us to have gracious speech: "Walk in wisdom toward outsiders, making the best use of the time. Let your speech always be gracious, seasoned with salt, so that you may know how you ought to answer each person" (Col. 4:5–6). He warns us against "corrupting talk" in Ephesians 4:29: "Let no corrupting talk come out of your mouths, but only such as is good for building up, as fits the occasion, that it may give grace to those who hear." And against foolish or crude talk one chapter later: "Let there be no filthiness nor foolish talk nor crude joking, which are out of place, but instead let there be thanksgiving" (Eph. 5:4).

And just in case we weren't clear, he spells it out in Colossians 3:8–9: "But now you must put them all away: anger, wrath, malice, slander, and obscene talk from your mouth. Do not lie to one another, seeing that you have put off the old self with its practices."

John warns us against being all talk: "Little children, let us not love in word or talk but in deed and in truth" (1 John 3:18). And Paul speaks of not relying on eloquent words, but on the cross of Christ in 1 Corinthians 1:17: "For Christ did not send me to baptize but to preach the gospel, and not with words of eloquent wisdom, lest the cross of Christ be emptied of its power." Or on flattery: "For we never came with words of flattery, as you know, nor with a pretext for greed—God is witness" (1 Thess. 2:5).

These commands are always in effect, with whomever we dialogue— along with, of course, the golden rule of Matthew 7:12: "So whatever you wish that others would do to you, do also to them, for this is the Law and the Prophets."

We are wise to abide by these instructions for every conversation, even over social media. These biblical principles inform our words even when our message is challenging or confrontational. By observing them, we eliminate many problematic speech issues before conversations get hard.

Think of hard conversations as the superhighway of speech. If we condition and train for them on the quiet back roads of ordinary, daily exchanges, we'll be in better verbal and spiritual shape to handle the challenges of tense situations.

ARTwork

Answer: When have you experienced the power of the tongue to "set ablaze"? Can you think of a time you received words from someone that were corrective but protective?

Read: James had much to say about the tongue. Read James 1:19–27 and 3:1–18. Write these verses in your own words.

Try: Hearing is believing. If you're like me, you spot examples of unbiblical speech easily enough but find it harder to spot "speech seasoned with salt," or talk that is "good for building up." I need living examples. Within your family, ministry team, or small group, post some biblical guidelines for speech in your meeting or common area, and when someone is exhibiting an example of godly speech, stop to acknowledge and appreciate it. This little habit of reinforcing good patterns will pay off in habit and culture change.

Lesson 2

No Peddlers, No Meddlers

*But let none of you suffer as a murderer or a thief
or an evildoer or as a meddler. (1 Peter 4:15)*

It's worth another reminder that not every impulse to engage in a hard conversation comes from God. Sometimes it's just our old meddling souls.

It's an inclination as natural as breathing to get all up in one another's business. While the premise of this book is that God does want us engaged in challenging conversations, He's clear that He wants our love informed by wisdom, not by nosiness or whim.

A kindly gentleman was overcome with compassion for his neighbors in the aftermath of 9/11. He wanted the owners of a local convenience store to feel safe and accepted. They were American citizens, but had immigrated from the Mideast, so this gentleman was afraid others weren't treating the couple well.

He dropped by the couple's store, purchased a dozen items in addition to his usual morning coffee, and told them they'd be welcome at his church anytime. The owners thanked him, and the gentleman felt good about the exchange.

As he pulled out, he noticed the store wasn't flying an American flag. Everyone was displaying flags in response to 9/11, so he decided that was a practical way he could serve the couple. He purchased a flag and gifted it to them the next day.

Day three, the gentleman arrived for his coffee. No flag. Five days passed, and the owners to whom he was showing the love of Christ appeared unwilling to utilize his gift (though, this gentleman never asked the reason directly). This is where the story takes an odd turn.

He heard a news anchorman encourage everyone, in the wake of the terrorism, to report suspicious behavior to Homeland Security. He drove to the convenience store and noted the still vacant flagpole. This time the gentleman reported the owners' lack of a flag to the authorities as suspicious behavior, making sure to explain they'd been given one, yet neglected to display it.

That's how Christians slide from ministering to meddling.

> ## Sometimes life's hardships are intended not to inspire us to acquire answers but to seek Jesus.

Now, meddling isn't the exclusive purview of Christians. I've been on the receiving end of interference from proselytizing vegans at the gym, overbearing moms on the playground, and neighbors who know exactly what I should do with my lawn. My daughter would occasionally ask her older brother for help with a tricky puzzle or math problem, only to find his assistance continue long after it was desired. "Mom!" she'd call out. "Zack's overhelping again."

It's a common affliction.

We need one another. We must be involved in one another's lives. But we Christians must take care not to overhelp or meddle.

Respect others as decision makers. Ask questions before assuming. Allow people to struggle sometimes. Encourage them to wrestle with the great questions of life and faith without prepackaging every answer. Sometimes life's hardships are intended not to inspire us to acquire answers but to seek Jesus.

> ## Ministering respects personal boundaries; meddling ignores them.

We represent the Savior, but we aren't the Savior. That *but* has enormous theological and practical significance. Overhelping can be as big a problem (and a distraction) as not helping at all. Healthy boundaries are important for healthy living. Ministering respects personal boundaries; meddling ignores them.

Each of us answers to God for our own lives. When lives intersect, even with our own children, it's rare that He intends us to assume all the decision making and life planning for another human.

Proceed with caution. Maintain perspective. We are children of the

Most High God, not hall monitors for Planet Earth. Even redeemed people can be tempted to be impulsive, overly critical, and quick to speak. Remembering we represent our Father, the King, will help us rein in our penchant for meddling. Because we represent Christ, we practice humility.

Jesus was known for humility, but I would wager that isn't a word that comes to mind about some Christians. Why doesn't our speech reflect a humble spirit?

First, we can't reflect humility in our speech if we don't have it in our hearts. God calls us to walk in humility with other believers (Eph. 4:1–3) and when we are being light to the world (Phil. 2:14–15). God sends plenty of humbling experiences our way, and we'd be wise to accept them with gratitude rather than dodge or dismiss them.

Second, it goes against our understanding of the world to practice sharing the story of our faith humbly from our hearts, as thirsty sinners who've found living water rather than know-it-all converts who've discovered all the answers. And yet it isn't our answers people need as much as they need our Lord.

I'd spent weeks having coffee with one coworker without once realizing she was Jewish. I'd been so busy talking about myself, I'd barely asked her a question. When she finally mentioned her Judaism, I was aghast.

"Wait, you're Jewish? I've gone on and on about my struggles as a Christian and my relationship with Jesus. Why didn't you ever stop me?" I asked.

She laughed. "You do go on and on. You might want to pause for air occasionally." Then she shrugged. "I have to admit, I was kind of studying you. All the other Christians I ever met acted sweet all the time and seemed to have every answer. You have real problems, and there's nothing sweet about you at all. That was refreshing. And, I confess, I'm starting to like your Jesus."

God used that exchange to encourage me to spend less time preaching and more time simply letting others into my life, being myself, and speaking naturally about my experience with Jesus.

People walking away from hearing the gospel shouldn't have the same feeling they do when walking away from a pyramid-scheme sales pitch.

We aren't God's public relations department, and we don't have a soul quota. People are miraculous creations of God, not our projects or statistics to quote during testimony time.

Or, as Paul put it, "For we are not, like so many, peddlers of God's word, but as men of sincerity, as commissioned by God, in the sight of God we speak in Christ" (2 Cor. 2:17).

ARTWORK

Answer: When has someone approached you with an uninvited suggestion for your life that worked out to be a positive experience? What made it useful, not meddling?

Read: There are limits to how much we can manage another person's life. In John 21:20–23, Peter asks Jesus about John's future. What is Jesus's answer?

Try: Focus on a calm presentation of the truth. We sometimes engage in conversations with others who aren't presenting facts. Pray for the Holy Spirit to reign, and calmly respond to untruths with relentless statements of truth. Notice the following conversation.

"You always think I'm lying."

"Not true. Many days I'm confident in your answers."

"You take my sister's side every time. I don't stand a chance."

"Not true. I'm always on the side of the facts, and this time, your story doesn't line up with the evidence."

"I guess you think I'm just a jerk all the time."

"Also not true. I love you and believe you have some wonderful qualities, but right now, we're discussing this one incident."

Lesson 3

The Whole Truth

*Rather, speaking the truth in love, we are
to grow up in every way into him who is
the head, into Christ. (Eph. 4:15)*

My friend's church was in the middle of a debate over contemporary music versus hymns. One Sunday, as soon as the contemporary set concluded, his pew mate (a hymn lover) emitted an exaggerated sigh and muttered, "Whew, I'm glad that's over."

This friend turned to her and calmly stated, "That is a very bad attitude," before returning to focus on the service. After the benediction, the woman responded. "Thank you for what you said. You were right. I had a bad attitude, and I'm sorry. What I said wasn't very loving toward our music team. The truth is, I don't like feeling left out of the music, but I need to see the notes to sing along. That's really what bothers me."

They resolved this by asking the music leader to supply her with copies of the sheet music going forward. She never felt left out of her own worship service again (and who wants that?). She'd uttered a comment in anger, but it wasn't the whole truth, which is something we should be alert to when anyone expresses anger or any of its relatives—frustration, irritation, and indignation. These feelings are generally just the tip of a greater iceberg. They're the "safe" feelings to express on behalf of the more vulnerable ones of fear, loneliness, or dejection.

Anger is just the warhead of an extensive and complex system of lurking emotions.

This woman expressed irritation when the whole truth included a sense of being excluded and "left behind" by a changing culture, as well as a fear that her "heart-music" for worship (essentially her first musical worship language) was disappearing. When my friend called her out with his simple, honest reflection, she wisely used it as an opportunity to turn the situation around and reveal the mountain of feelings lurking just beneath her gripe.

It's often easier to let people complain and snipe. We write them off as "church or office cranks" and dismiss them. Harder is to hear them out, prod them to reveal what's behind the frustration, and engage in a longer discussion about their needs and healthier ways to express them. But be warned. Complaining is a contagion. Anger is just the warhead of an extensive and complex system of lurking emotions.

If, rather than avoid the complainers in our midst, we listen to them and have our own conversation about growing up in Christ by obeying Philippians 2:14–18, the whole body would be the better for it. This is also important to do with coworkers or family who make no claim to faith in Christ. They may not see the Bible as an authority in their lives, but by taking time to probe beneath their anger and redirect them to healthier expressions, we serve them well too.

This is one way we live out Hebrews 12:14–15: "Strive for peace with everyone, and for the holiness without which no one will see the Lord. See to it that no one fails to obtain the grace of God; that no 'root of bitterness' springs up and causes trouble, and by it many become defiled."

Sometimes we imagine that the loving thing to do is to avoid speaking truth. But that isn't always the wisest choice.

A few years ago, I sat beside a frustrated gentleman who had once been deeply involved in a ministry, but now found himself set aside, excluded, without explanation. I'd heard the talk. People felt that while he had great enthusiasm, he wasn't good at that work.

The problem was, no one discussed this with him. They just found ways to push him aside, and so, there we sat, him with his head in his hands and lots of questions. I agreed with their assessment of his skills, but saw the damage done by not telling him.

It wasn't my place to have the conversation. I considered saying nothing, but that felt cruel to him. Then I thought about telling him I'd overheard the others say he wasn't very good. That felt like gossip and a setup for conflict.

After praying, I chose to ask questions to help focus his thoughts. "Mike, how do you feel about your abilities for this ministry?"

He stared at the ground. "I thought I was good at it. I love it, and in my spiritual gifts class, the teacher said that's one of the indications that we're gifted in that area."

"Did he mention other indicators?"

Mike thought for a moment. "Yeah, a few. Like fruitfulness. If our work produces fruit, that's a good sign. I know the ministry was falling off. Is that about fruit? Honestly, I don't even know what fruitfulness is."

I laughed. "That's a good insight. Any other indicators?"

He nodded. "He also said 'outside confirmation.' Other people believe you're gifted for that area. Do other people think I'm not gifted for this?"

"That's a great question to ask people who've worked with you. Have you ever told the leaders you'd like their thoughts on your gifts?"

"Wow, no. I just kept doing it. I'd want to know if I was bad at it. I mean, there's other things I can do. If I'm not good at it, though, wouldn't they just tell me?"

I shrugged, knowing no one had. "Not everyone has the courage to engage in hard conversations, like telling a person they aren't gifted for ministry. Sometimes they think it's unloving to say something like that."

"It's a lot more unloving to leave me wondering why they didn't ask me back."

I agree.

We can extend compassion to all parties in this situation. This behavior is a fallout, for the most part, of well-intentioned Christians not wanting to be "that church." We don't want to be some distorted image in Satan's funhouse mirror of the worst examples of Christians, hurting others with words. Instead, we must defy his evil plan and declare that his distortion will not inhibit us from exercising God's truth.

> **Withholding truth leaves a vacuum for deception to enter and fill a space intended for God's truth.**

Unfortunately, to avoid that snare, we sometimes withhold the truth. And that's what it is—withholding truth. Right there, that doesn't sound like Christ, does it? In fact, withholding truth leaves a vacuum for deception to enter and fill a space intended for God's truth.

Christians are called to deliver the truth—the whole truth—even when the entire scope of that truth includes information that is unpleasant, challenging, or uncomfortable.

Keep in mind the interrelationship between truth and love. Truth is nonnegotiable for the speech of believers. Our words must always be grounded in it. There's no place for deception in Christians' conversations. But truth can be like tofu. It has its own nature and consistency, yet still takes on the flavor of the other elements with which it's served.

The New Testament writers knew that if we dish up truth with sarcasm, anger, malice, slander, or a side of empty words, it becomes unpalatable. If, however, we serve truth alongside grace, wisdom, and thanksgiving on a fresh bed of love, then it becomes a feast for hungry souls. Truth, like chicken soup, has healing powers, but served cold, it becomes an unkindness and harder to swallow.

So, we understand there are comprehensive truths that guide all the activity of believers. And because we represent Jesus, we must maintain integrity regarding truth and love. These are the guardrails of hard conversations that keep us traveling in the "safe" lane during hard conversations. By "safe," I mean we're operating from a place of biblical obedience; not safe means we're guaranteed a specific or painless outcome. Truth and love keep us on the narrow road when speaking with others.

ARTwork

Answer: Who are the best people to speak hard truth to you? What qualifies them to say hard things?

Read: Read Ephesians 4:1–16 and then rewrite it in your own words or create art that reflects what it says.

Try: We change best in a supportive environment with regular opportunities to practice new skills we hope will become habits. Any small group situation can become a vehicle for culture change. Schedule ten to fifteen minutes of your meeting, family meal, or Bible study to practice a skill for improved communication. Skills that lend themselves to this are reflection, open-ended questions, and summarizing.

Lesson 4

Did God Really Say?

Now the serpent was more crafty than any other beast of the field that the LORD God had made. He said to the woman, "Did God actually say, 'You shall not eat of any tree in the garden'?" (Gen. 3:1)

For years I taught a weekly Bible study for female black belt students. Many hadn't read the Bible before we began.

Our practice was to attend karate class and then retire to one of their homes for study. These were bright, provocative women who helped me have an entirely new perspective on Scriptures I'd studied many times. They were also impatient and would start discussing the material during karate class. Sometimes they'd shout questions across the dojo floor as forty people trained.

This presented some challenges. Working with a partner on a block or kick, suddenly I'd hear, "Hey, Lori! The Bible says it's wrong to be gay, doesn't it?" or "Lori, abortion is murder, but doesn't God forgive murderers?" They tested my turtle self almost beyond bearing. My default reply was, "That's not something I'll discuss between a block and a throw."

One time, one of the men partnered with me for a punching drill asked, "Hey there, Lori. Would you explain exactly what section of the Bible inspired my girlfriend to tell me we can't sleep together anymore because it's not biblical?" (I never imagined needing to increase my life insurance to lead a women's Bible study.)

Rarely have I invested such comprehensive preparation as I did for those ladies. I studied every topic that arose. Theological questions flew from all sides, and I wanted to be ready with biblically informed truth. These women brought the same rigor they loved in karate to our study, and it was a boon to us all.

Know the complete biblical story, not just a fuzzy headline.

Whenever we engage in a conversation about a hard topic, it's paramount to know the complete biblical story, not just a fuzzy headline. Hard conversations arise over issues of lifestyle and sin, questions of suffering and death, and on differences in theology among other things. Launching into any of these topics without sufficient understanding can cause more harm than help.

This doesn't mean we need to have theology degrees in every topic, but we ought to know why we believe what we do and where to find topics in Scripture. Mark 12:30 says that God wants us to love Him with everything we have, our minds included: "And you shall love the Lord your God with all your heart and with all your soul and with all your mind and with all your strength."

We've probably all encountered someone who spouted "biblical" insight that wasn't so biblical. In my twenties, I briefly dated a young African American man. An older family friend visiting from out of state disapproved. "You're asking for trouble, Lori Ann. The Bible says, 'Birds of a feather, flock together.'"

I shook my head. "It absolutely does not say that."

She was undeterred. "Well, somewhere it says, 'Seek ye your own kind, one to another.'"

"Nope. Not Scripture."

She stamped her foot and waved a finger at me. "Listen to your elders. It says that somewhere in Hezekiah."

> **Before offering faith-based comfort, counsel, or correction, we honor God and serve others best by checking to be sure what we offer is scripturally informed.**

Wrong on all counts. It's dizzying how often cultural counsel gets passed off as Scripture. Before offering faith-based comfort, counsel, or correction, we honor God and serve others best by checking to be sure what we offer is scripturally informed.

This can be done many ways. The best, in my opinion, is to make a habit of personal Bible reading. Seek continual learning from quality preachers and teachers. Study at least one book a year on biblical topics of interest.

Check with mature Christians in your community for quality web-sites that offer teaching on cultural topics. Purchase a topical Bible and befriend the staff at your local Christian bookstore. They can often direct you to a reliable book on any subject.

To check those phrases we think are biblical, but aren't sure, there are print and online concordances (books that list every word in the Bible and where to find it) that help us check where it may (or may not) be found in Scripture.

It's also acceptable to say, "I don't know if I understand that topic well enough to discuss it with you right now, but give me a week. Then, let's talk."

There's a difference, of course, between biblical truth and personal perspective.

For some hard conversations, the biblical foundation will be clear-cut: "Alberto, I've received word of your affair. God has a higher standard for married Christians." "Mom, you're talking behind Latoya's back. Gossip violates how God wants us to treat others."

> ## God's Word is unchanging; community and cultural standards shift with situations and times.

While these are still challenging, uncomfortable conversations, at least the biblical principle is clear. Other conversations may center on a biblical concept, but the details have more to do with perspective or community standards. God's Word is unchanging; community and cultural standards shift with situations and times.

If there are specific expectations in your community or ministry team and a person has violated them, it's appropriate to have a hard conversation, but be clear from the opening sentence that you're discussing a biblically informed community standard, not a specific biblical command. This clarity can eliminate confusion and sets parameters for a healthier discussion.

Conversations also improve when we verify information to be certain we're dealing with facts. This is part of making sure what we're saying is true. When my daughter was four, she had an imaginary penguin friend named Louie. He generally appeared when my husband traveled. Louie was a nuisance around the house. As in "Mom! You forgot to set a place for Louie," or "Zack! You just sat on Louie."

One Sunday I asked Hannah's Sunday school teacher if Louie had made any appearances in class.

Startled, she asked, "In class? My, no! Who is Louie, anyway?"

As I explained, she grew red-faced. "I'm so thankful you told me. A couple of us have been praying about talking with you, because Hannah always talks about 'Louie—who comes to stay with us when Daddy's out of town.'"

We chuckled over it, but as I walked away, I wondered exactly how many people had been praying for me and preparing for "a chat" about my mysterious male visitor.

> **Christians ask questions before accusing. We investigate before we interrogate. We research before we rebuke.**

Facts are our friends. Christians deal in truths—not deception, fallacies, or half-truths. We don't gossip or pass on hearsay. We have no place spreading online or email rumors without verification. Nor do we engage in hard conversations without investigating facts.

Christians ask questions before accusing. We investigate before we interrogate. We research before we rebuke.

This has historically been a problem with immature believers locally, but it's magnified now with the prevalence of social media. Far too many of us have engaged in circular and fruitless social media discussions based on "news" that turned out to be false. Even when it's a well-intentioned plea for prayer for some unverified atrocity happening on the other side of the world, it's wrong to spread a story without making sure it's true.

Facts are also practical for preventing panic. Whether it's a potential personal disaster or a possible global event, it's best to review what we know for certain over what "may" happen or "could be" happening.

Did Aunt Stacy's doctor say she has cancer, or is that *one* of the things for which she's testing? Is there proof that a terrorist group has infiltrated Texas, or is that an Internet rumor? Is our pastor suffering from Alzheimer's, or is he getting forgetful and we don't know why?

Christians traffic in truth. Period. Every time we compromise this, even in small ways, we detract from our integrity and bring into question the trustworthiness of Christ.

ARTwork

Answer: List phrases you hear Christians use that are not from the Bible. Are there alternates people could substitute that are actually biblical?

Read: Psalm 12 will resonate with many of us. What does this Psalm say about the words of the godless as compared to the words of the Lord?

Try: Record and sign. For many reasons, people become confused about what's been said during hard conversations. My parents began to argue about what they heard their doctors instruct. They started taking notes during medical appointments and asking the physician to read and initial their notes. This settled much confusion.

This is also useful during tense conversations. It doesn't have to be detailed or lengthy, but at the end of the discussion, simply write what's been agreed to (or not) and have the participants read it and sign to verify this is what they recall being discussed. It's a helpful tool for confusing situations, people with mental or hearing challenges, and as a guard against unscrupulous people who may report something different following a hard conversation.

HEART OF THE ART PRACTICE

Research one biblical topic people in your life discuss. Choose one you don't currently feel qualified to defend.

Is This Conversation Grounded and Timed in Love?

Lesson 1

The Love Questions

Above all, keep loving one another earnestly, since love covers a multitude of sins. (1 Peter 4:8)

I was surprised when Carly invited me to lunch.

Our church had been experiencing a conflict that had divided many. Carly and I had had numerous hard conversations about her attitude. Our last conversation had been particularly adversarial, so I was nervous that our meeting might be a vengeful ambush.

Carly arrived after I did, and once we ordered, she didn't keep me in suspense. "I need your help and your prayers. My doctor called me to discuss my most recent test results, and I don't want to face it alone. Can you come along?"

I was taken aback. "Of course. Still, I'm surprised you're asking me."

"Why?" she said, leaning back in the booth.

"Well, our last few exchanges haven't been the most comfortable," I replied.

She nodded. "In fact, I hated those conversations. But through everything, one thing that's always been clear is that you love me. It takes a huge commitment to love to stick with someone through talks like that.

Other people probably have thought those things and just given up on me or walked away. I'll take the tough talks as long as there's the love."

Love is a multidimensional quality. It's both a noun, representing a feeling, and a verb, representing actions that put others first. In John 21, after Jesus has risen from the dead, He appears to some of the disciples on the shore of the Sea of Tiberias. In verses 15–19, over breakfast, Jesus asks Peter three times about his love for Him. Peter answers three times that he does, indeed, love Jesus. Jesus's response to each affirmative answer is to call Peter to action—feeding Jesus's sheep—in demonstration of this love.

> **To say that we love others is to say we're willing to risk our own discomfort to speak hard things to them.**

To say that we love Jesus is to say we are ready to obey Him by living and speaking the truth. To say that we love Jesus is to say we are willing to reflect Him by loving and serving others. To say that we love others is to say we're willing to risk our own discomfort to speak hard things to them. Love is a feeling that leads to action.

When we prepare for any hard conversation, we must ask ourselves questions about love. Do I love this person, and if not, what am I going to do about that? Am I being loving to speak this truth in this way, at this time, to this person?

Some believers falsely assume (and teach) that to be loving means to stay silent about truth or compromise it in some way. Others are so afraid that loving feelings will lead to a softening of truth, they harden their hearts toward others and eschew mercy. This is dangerous thinking—both for the church of Jesus Christ and ultimately for the world.

> **Love and truth can occupy the same space, just as surely as Christ was fully human and fully God.**

The world (meaning people who don't follow Jesus) has absconded with love, replacing God's idea of love with a facsimile that many buy as the real thing. And not just the world. Some parts of the body of Christ believe that to be loving, biblical truth must be muted or modified.

Not so. Jesus walked on Earth living out perfect love while delivering perfect truth. It is possible. It's not possible without Jesus, but it's possible. Love and truth can occupy the same space, just as surely as Christ was fully human and fully God.

I'm aware that these two words frustrate, frighten, or trigger a wound reflex in some people. We've heard this phrase before, perhaps tossed around the church like a beach ball (or a dodge ball).

"I'm just speaking the truth in love, is all."

"Well, don't you know you have to speak truth in love?"

Intended for useful instruction, this power-filled phrase from Ephesians 4 is too often snapped from its context like a tree branch and used to club innocent passersby in Jesus's name. The misguided speaker is often leaning heavily toward a personal interpretation of truth, while offering only a passing nod at anything others might recognize as love.

Inhale. Exhale. There's no way to write a book about hard conversations without filling it with a few, and this is one.

It's tempting to edit from Scripture any passage that's been misused, but this would be detrimental (not to mention heretical). Agreed, there has been a shameful amount of bullying that's occurred in Jesus's name. This speaking the truth in love concept has too often been the last word spiritually bludgeoned victims hear just before they hit the mat.

> **The worst thing we can do . . . is to allow the bullies and abusers the last word on God's Word.**

The worst thing we can do, though—worse than lancing the wounds—is to allow the bullies and abusers the last word on God's Word. It will challenge some of us to revisit "speaking the truth in love," but these are our Father's words. We must reclaim them from the bullies.

Of course, we can fairly represent love and truth simultaneously. Parents do it with children every day. Spouses do it. Church leaders, doctors, friends, and others all speak truth and communicate love, sometimes in the same breath.

When I say love, I am not referring to the world's diluted version. What I mean is love as defined by God in 1 Corinthians 13:4–8: "Love is patient and kind; love does not envy or boast; it is not arrogant or rude. It does not insist on its own way; it is not irritable or resentful; it does not rejoice at wrongdoing, but rejoices with the truth. Love bears all things, believes all things, hopes all things, endures all things. Love never ends."

When we ask the questions, "Do I love this person?" and "Is this conversation grounded and timed in love?" we need to ask them in the "amplified" version. Replace the word *love* with its definition.

"Am I being patient, kind, not envious or boastful, humble, not rude when I speak this truth? Am I insisting on my own way or being irritable and resentful? Am I rejoicing, even a little bit, in someone's wrongdoing or trouble? Am I willing to bear with that person, believe, hope, endure, and offer a love that doesn't end?"

By doing this, we see what practices and attitudes demonstrate godly love.

> **We need to be trained and transformed by love, so that love is our first language, our initial reflex, and our emotional default setting.**

Love is our high calling. The highest. We need to be trained and transformed by love, so that love is our first language, our initial reflex, and our emotional default setting. We need to foster loving hearts, if we want that love to influence our words.

Humanity can produce a pleasant enough facsimile—a pseudo love that lasts a pretty long time and feels pretty good. But human love runs out. We exhaust it. We modify it. It wears thin, falls off, and dies. The good news is that Jesus is the inexhaustible source of pure, eternal love—a love that is stronger than death.

When we reflect on our love factor before engaging in a hard conversation, we may discover we don't love this person. We may, in fact, have downright unloving feelings and thoughts regarding that person or situation. That's not an excuse to avoid the conversation—instead, it's an opportunity to tap into the deep love of Jesus (before we speak) and thus, grow up a little more into Him.

Do I love this person? When we're talking about having hard conversations about death, divorce, addiction, behavior change, or life events with family or friends, this is an easy question to answer. It doesn't make stressful conversations any easier, but we know that we love the other soul involved.

Where it gets harder is asking this love question about people outside our inner circle. This calling to speak the truth in love includes the truth-telling we do to people we don't know. But how are we supposed to love someone we barely know or perhaps haven't even met?

The answer is simple to state—hard to live. We must exercise every opportunity to practice love, while weeding out all attitudes or behaviors that interfere with it. Harboring hatred, envy, pride, vengeance, greed, fear, or other sinful attitudes diminishes our capacity for love and prevents us from hearing one another clearly.

I live in a small town. Some of my full-time work has been with families referred for help by the Department of Children, Youth, and Families. DCYF can ignite fear in families.

Once, I was halfway up the deck stairs of a home in my own town when a screaming woman emerged from the slider doors holding two snarling pit bulls on leashes. "Get in your car and drive straight back to the city, you! We don't need state workers here. You people don't understand us here. Go away, or I'll let go of these leashes."

Suddenly my legs just wouldn't work. I glanced at my car far down her dirt driveway, and knew I was in trouble. Immediately, I shouted my credentials as a local over the growling canines. I was trying to make any personal connection I could make. "I'm not from upstate. I live here. I grew up in this town."

"You can't trick me!" she shouted and let some slack on the leashes.

"No, honest. My dad's the fire chief. I was Lori Stanley. I'm from here." My words came out as fast as my heart pounded.

"What? Stanley? As in Chief Stanley? Why didn't you say so?" At once, the dogs were caged, I was gulping iced tea, regaining feeling in my extremities, and this family welcomed the help they needed.

We all unleash internal snarling dogs when we encounter someone who threatens us on some level. The barking may make it harder to hear what the other is saying. By making a connection on some level, we can, like this woman did, silence our dogs long enough to converse. Seek that connecting place. Find the common ground.

My college professor used to say that when we meet someone very different from us, we must remember that they too bear the Creator's thumbprint, having been made in His image. Ask God to help you see that print, even if at first you must take it on faith that it is there.

Whatever is a barrier to love must be met with faith that Christ can defeat it and replace it with a quality that is hospitable to love. As we increase in our capacity to love others, we will increase in the qualities listed in 1 Corinthians 13. Those qualities, combined with truth, are the backbone of fruitful hard conversations.

ARTwork

Answer: How do you know when someone loves you earnestly?

Read: 1 Peter 4:7–11 instructs us to love one another "earnestly." Other translations use words such as "deeply," "fervently," "constantly," and "sincerely." What do these verses say about what that looks like?

Try: Work on your social media graces. Some wise guidelines for interacting online include the following: (a) only write and share verifiable truth, (b) only write what you would speak face-to-face, (c) remember people not in the conversation are watching, and (d) we'll be held accountable for words in tweets and status updates just as we will for words spoken one-on-one, so let's live up to our calling at all times.

Lesson 2

What If I Lack Love?

If I speak in the tongues of men and of
angels, but have not love, I am a noisy gong
or a clanging cymbal. (1 Cor. 13:1)

What happens if we ask ourselves if we love the other person and we realize our answer is no? Or not as well as we should? Or we used to love that person, but now we're not sure? Or we thought we loved that person, but he or she isn't feeling it and we're not acting on it? For Christians, there's a remedy.

A pastor friend once told me he came to realize he didn't love the people he was called to lead. God showed him how much of his ministry was focused on his own development at the expense of those he'd come to serve. I also once found myself sitting in a conference room realizing I didn't love my coworkers enough to pray for them regularly or to share the truth of Christ with them. For both of us, the solution began with honest assessment, confession, and prayer.

> **Love, as we know, isn't all about a feeling, but it isn't not a feeling either.**

Love, as we know, isn't all about a feeling, but it isn't not a feeling either. Take another look at Paul's description of love in 1 Corinthians 13:4–7. This passage touches on actions and attitudes. It mentions feelings but reaches beyond them. When we're considering a hard conversation with someone, whether it be a subordinate at work, our father-in-law, a wayward child, or an antagonistic neighbor, it is wise to measure our inner attitude and outward actions against this passage.

Or consider the apostle John's words in 1 John 3:11–18, where he describes the demonstration of God's love in laying down His life for us and commands us to do the same for our brothers. The call to love isn't about holding hands and singing around a campfire. It's about laying down our lives—as well as our agendas, comforts, defenses, and bad attitudes.

The love-answer for my pastor friend and for me came initially in the form of daily prayer for others. Investing this time in them was the first act of love that engaged us before our feelings came in line.

Then we asked God to help us see others with His eyes and love them with His love. This led both of us, independently, to begin listening to people and caring about their stories.

One day this pastor, who had previously felt saddened by the hardness of his heart, found himself weeping over his congregation as he prayed. He isn't a weeping man, but it was a sign to him that he was making progress with love.

It would be a subject of concern if I sat at my day job weeping over coworkers. For me, the changes came about in my willingness to put their needs ahead of my own, and to seek small ways to serve them. I too am growing in love.

We have different roles in people's lives. A wife asking for a renewed love for her husband is going to be seeking a different expression of that than a marine sergeant asking for a love for his troops. But I've yet to see a passage in Scripture that exempts any of us from loving anyone. The opening verse of 1 Corinthians 13 is a sobering warning that we can get all the words right and yet be nothing more than clanging cymbals without love.

So, how do we increase in love?

This isn't about being "nice"; it's about being like Jesus.

First, we study God's Word to remind ourselves of God's definition of love. Our minds can become polluted by the world's diluted notion of love, but Song of Solomon 8:6 tells us that "love is strong as death." This isn't about being "nice"; it's about being like Jesus. Immerse yourself in what the Bible says love looks like.

Second, ask God to examine your heart regarding love in general, but also toward specific subjects of hard conversation. Do you love others as well as you could be loving them? If you're not sure, ask a trusted, mature, believing friend to evaluate your ability to love. Then listen.

Third, ask God to give you His love with which to love others. Peter tells us in 2 Peter 1:1–11 to make every effort to supplement our faith with several qualities, among them love. The implication of this passage is that we can increase in love and should do so to be effective and fruitful as believers.

Fourth, do the things love does. Until your feelings line up with your faith, act in loving ways toward others as described by God's Word. One of my friends told of a time when his largely Caucasian suburban church felt God's call to reach out to a nearby inner-city church, comprised mostly of African American Christians.

It was a season of riots in the city, and their congregation wanted to do what they could to repair race relations, so they invited the urban church to join in worship. The response of the urban congregation was straightforward—if you want to love us, come into the city to worship with us. They did, and this began a powerful journey of reconciliation for both congregations. Both groups of believers fumbled on the way to learning to love one another. Still, they began by loving imperfectly and let God teach them better along the way.

There are times when, just as we can have a lapse in judgment, we can find we've had a lapse in love. The love problem isn't that we don't love; it's that we've lost sight of that love and fallen into the habit of behaving in unloving ways. This can happen even with our own families when love for self overshadows love for others.

A lack of (or lapse in) love doesn't excuse us from having hard conversations, but it should slow us down. Love is a nonnegotiable with God. It's not a luxury or an optional strategy. When you must engage in hard conversations, but recognize you're facing a love deficit, consider taking some steps to scaffold you as God refills you with love.

- Invite an individual with a clear sense of love for the other person to witness your conversation and give you frank feedback on your word and tone choices.
- Admit to the other person that you've recognized you have work to do in the area of love. Say something like, "I can see I haven't been expressing love in meaningful ways to you lately." Or "God is helping me see that I could be more loving toward some of the people I serve. I'd like the chance to do better."
- Arrange to do an activity with the other person before you schedule a hard conversation. This could be social such as attending a movie, having dinner, or playing basketball. Or it could be a

project such as raking leaves for an elderly neighbor, cleaning up a vacant lot near the office, or bringing your dogs to read with children at the local youth center. This time focused on serving others together or enjoying a shared activity can open doors for you to relax with each other and build a basis on which love can grow (or be renewed).

ARTwork

Answer: What's the hardest thing about admitting you lack love for someone or have lost sight of your love for someone else?

Read: In John 13:31–35 Jesus issues a new commandment that his disciples love one another just as He has loved them. List the ways that Jesus loves us.

Try: Read Proverbs 16. At the end of every day for one week, consider one conversation you had and ask yourself what your feelings are toward that person. Consider how emotions affected your conversation. What insights do you gain by doing this? What might have been different if you'd done it before your chat? Is there room for growth in loving this person?

Lesson 3

Love Waits (Sometimes)

Wait for the LORD;
be strong, and let your heart take courage;
wait for the LORD!
(Ps. 27:14)

Turtle mode is sometimes the right stance to take when it comes to hard conversations. There is a timing piece to demonstrating love when confronting others with tough truth. The moment we have the urge to speak up isn't always the moment to let words emerge. It's wise to, at least, take time to pray and ask God to make the timing clear.

In ongoing relationships or with people who are likely to be in our lives for a significant period of time, it's profitable to ask God to prepare their hearts for a discussion of the topic. Pray that God gives them ears to hear. Pray through the six questions described here. And pray for God to open a natural (or supernatural) opportunity for conversation.

The moment we have the urge to speak up isn't always the moment to let words emerge.

One of my part-time jobs was in a fitness center. We had a crowd of older members who worked out daily, and it was on my heart to share the gospel with many of them. I prayed regularly for God to soften their hearts and to give me eyes to see natural opportunities for these talks. In the meantime, I listened to them and found little ways to serve them.

A constant in the fitness room was the news channel. One morning we arrived to the news that an anchor from their favorite program had died unexpectedly of sudden cardiac death. In processing the sad development, multiple members asked me spiritual questions and shared their own fears about what might happen after death. Over the next three weeks, I was able to share the gospel with nearly all of them in a way that felt natural to them and to me.

Timing doesn't always just present itself. If, after prayer, it's clear that we're the person to have this conversation, it's biblical, and we've worked through the questions, we may schedule a time to chat. I found it best not to ambush people and am sure to let them know at the invitation that I'd like to discuss an important matter, usually previewing the topic of discussion so they have time to prepare. This demonstrates love, respect, and faith that even if they put up defenses, God can overcome them in His time.

Sometimes hawks are right too, though. There are God moments when even with very little relationship with a person or little time to prepare, we're the ones called to open our mouths with a timely message.

When my friend finally died of her brain tumor, a group of us gathered at the convalescent home where she'd spent her last days. One of her friends, a new believer, arrived with her husband, who, as it turns out, was an old acquaintance of mine, one I hadn't seen in over fifteen years.

We sat together weeping and sharing memories. At one point, my old friend leaned over and commented that he'd been to many wakes, but there was something different about the way we mourned.

I prayed silently before answering. "We're devastated that she's gone from us, but we know for certain she's with Jesus. Are you a Christian?"

"Nah. I know it's probably true, but I'm not ready to take that step. I guess I'm waiting for that last moment before I die, like the thief on the cross," he replied.

Maybe it was the shock of her death, but I was so taken aback by his insistence on taking time for granted, I responded with an urgent, confident tone quite unlike my turtle self.

"Do you see where we're sitting? What makes you think you're going to have a 'thief on the cross' moment? You're not guaranteed anything. Our friend thought she'd have more time, but here we are. This is your moment, not some other. You could leave here and die on the ride home. Why wait? Decide about Jesus right now."

I shocked myself (and the friends listening in) with both my long-winded speech and the urgency of my tone. But what shocked everyone more was that he accepted Jesus that day.

> **Just as our electronic devices must align themselves with the international atomic clock, so we must align our spirits to God's timing.**

This was God's timing, not mine. I was grieving and didn't "feel" especially in tune with God's Holy Spirit, but I'm grateful God used me. I was just the person present in that place at that time.

Just as our electronic devices must align themselves with the international atomic clock, so we must align our spirits to God's timing. Sometimes the Spirit says wait when we're overeager to go. Other times He says move now, when we'd be just as happy to stand still.

Work through the questions (or flip through them if time is short), allow love to rule, and ask, "Is this conversation grounded and timed in love?"

There are situations that have a timeliness factor. The moment presents itself, and it must be redeemed or missed. When time isn't an immediate factor, though, we can take other dynamics into consideration.

For example, we want to let our children know about our cancer diagnosis, but one of them is scheduled for a major exam or has an imminent special event. We may choose to delay our conversation so as not to further complicate an important moment in their lives.

Or we know we want to confront our pastor, but maybe Sunday between services isn't the kindest timing.

Or maybe we know the most loving thing is to wait so that we can involve someone else in the conversation. The church is a body, and there are times to work as a team, not a solitary agent of truth.

Would Dad hear the gospel better from one of his peers who follows Jesus? That doesn't mean we ignore the prompting, but perhaps we could invite him and his believing friend out to dinner. Maybe one of his other children is better suited to share with him right now. Our role may be to call our sibling and plant the seed.

Or what about that teenager in the church whose behavior is worrying us? Are we the right person to remark about her new tattoos and purple hair, or would this be the first exchange she's ever had with us? If we don't know anything else about her life, maybe the best action is to befriend her before we voice our concern. Or maybe God is impressing on us to pray for the right person to engage in this conversation.

As in all things, God's timing and teaming is best. Out of love for Him and for others, we do well to consult Him on both.

ARTWORK

Answer: When have you been the "victim" of an ill-timed conversation? When has a conversation come to you at just the right time?

Read: The book of Esther is a study in timing. Read chapters 5 and 6. Notice that Esther didn't jump immediately to the hard conversation with the king even though danger was imminent. What was God working out in the time Esther waited?

Try: Pray for the person you've had in mind for a hard conversation. Pray for that person to have ears that hear. Ask God to provide you opportunities to serve the person and a natural opportunity to speak up.

HEART OF THE ART PRACTICE

When Hawks Gather

In every group, there's likely to be a combination of hawks and turtles. It can be challenging for leaders to keep a lid on the hawks and draw out the turtles. One important tool is the poll. Turtles appreciate a warning, so several minutes prior to doing this, let the group know it's coming. It would sound something like this.

"The topic we're discussing is so important, I'm going to do two or three polls or check-ins tonight. In five minutes, I'm going to go around the room and ask everyone for thoughts on question two."

Then, begin with a hawk and go around the room, encouraging everyone to speak. Give the time-out sign or point to your watch if anyone goes long.

The key elements of an effective poll are (a) forewarning and (b) monitoring time limits so everyone is comfortable speaking. Making a habit of the poll helps turtles relax with hawks because they know they won't have to fight for airtime. Turtles appreciate invitations to speak, and hawks benefit from opportunities to listen.

Vulnerability Works for Turtles

Vulnerability is the turtle's best friend. The hardest part of a hard conversation for a turtle is often starting it, so don't delay. Time is a turtle's enemy. The moment you sit down with the other person, dive into the subject, but be vulnerable.

It may sound like this.

"I invited you here because I care. I'm really nervous. I don't feel as though I'm good at talking to others about God, but that's not because I don't believe that God is real. You've been going through a lot, and I want you to know God loves you and cares about what you're facing. I hope it's all right that I pray for you."

Or "I apologize right off the bat that I'm not great at explaining what the Bible says about hard topics. I trust my pastor, not blindly, but because he's proven himself to be trustworthy. I know what he teaches about homosexuality, and part of that is how much God loves everyone. He teaches that hate isn't acceptable for Christians, but he also teaches that homosexual behavior is biblically wrong. I care about you and I'd never want you to be hurt, but I believe the Bible is God's Word. Your life is your business, but I feel as if you want me to say I accept your lifestyle, and I can't. I'm uncomfortable telling you that, but I feel dishonest staying quiet."

Your running mental dialogue of nervousness or awkwardness can be your friend. Speak it aloud and let others see your vulnerability. They won't all respond in a positive way, but many will. Let God be your protector and defender. He does it best.

What's My Plan for Following Up Either Success or Rejection?

Lesson 1

Plans A and B

I therefore, a prisoner for the Lord, urge you to walk in a manner worthy of the calling to which you have been called, with all humility and gentleness, with patience, bearing with one another in love, eager to maintain the unity of the Spirit in the bond of peace. (Eph. 4:1–3)

A hard conversation may be the first step down a long, demanding road. Some hard conversations are single events. Others must be repeated or followed up. We almost never know at the outset, so it's important to count the cost before we engage in a hard conversation.

What are we willing to invest in the follow-up? How far down the path of change are we willing to walk with the other person? What if you knew you would have to have the same hard conversation with a person *for several years*?

I worked with a chronically homeless dad for about ten years. He wouldn't make the hard choices it took to obtain and maintain a job and a residence. He and his children bounced from relative to friend, sleeping on floors or in spare beds.

Whenever our paths crossed, he'd ask for help, and we'd have the same hard conversation. There is help available, but he'd have to make the choice to cooperate with the people and programs providing it.

Occasionally he'd try, but it wouldn't take long, often under a week, for him to text "I can't take these rules," or "I don't want people in my business." Next thing, he'd disappear.

Finally, one year he resurfaced, and I detected a change in attitude. He called me after exhausting every other support. "This is it," he said. "I have no place else to go. Will you help me?"

I launched into my spiel, but this time, he listened. He acted. He worked with me and cooperated with a program designed to help homeless families. One night, when he'd maintained a residence for over a month, he texted me. "Thank you for sticking with me. I'm going to make this work and show my children we can build a home."

> **People change according to their complex internal schedules, not always according to our concerted, external pressures.**

People change according to their complex internal schedules, not always according to our concerted, external pressures. Some people take longer than others, exhaustingly longer. Initially, we can't imagine they'll ever come around, but some do.

People mature. They weary of wrong paths. They find motivation. One key piece of information comes into perspective. Or the prayers of loved ones finally penetrate their darkness.

Other people, however, will refuse to change, and this can have important implications for the follow-up we invest after our conversation. We don't usually know which people will eventually change and which will refuse to change for their entire lives, so many of our decisions about follow-up will be based on the nature of our relationship, their behavior, and the leading of the Holy Spirit.

Clearly, a conversation with family is one we're likely to continue following closely. Whether we're sharing bad news, confronting on an area of growth, or explaining the gospel, we're likely to have numerous natural opportunities to check in with them once our initial conversation ends.

If, however, we're confronting a family member or close friend over a behavior we can't tolerate such as drug use, adultery, drinking, untreated mental illness, or physical abuse, we should have two plans ready.

Our first plan is one that we employ when we believe the person might be willing to change, or when we're engaged in a long-term relationship (family, coworker, church member), and the topic of conversation is regarding a character issue that isn't directly endangering that person or others.

For example, maybe our spouse has a short temper. Her anger isn't representative of Christ, but she's never resorted to violence. Or one of our church members displays no interest in reading the Bible or in praying. Or a coworker is antagonistic to our faith but not in any threatening way.

If we were going to have conversations with these people about these issues, we would prayerfully plan ways we could support them if they respond positively. This can be as simple as agreeing to pray for them or offering them a book or Bible study on the topic. Or it can include meeting regularly to encourage the other person's plan for change, perhaps including a pastor or spiritual guide in the conversation. It can go even deeper and involve a commitment to discipleship or babysitting so the person can attend a Bible class or becoming a friend, so that person has a better understanding of the Christian life just by knowing a Christian.

We can validate and affirm forward growth while displaying patience and forgiveness during stumbles.

Occasionally, the Holy Spirit enables one of us to change "overnight." I've known people who came to Christ and instantly lost their taste for alcohol, immediately dropped their cursing habit, or were instantly free of anger. However, many of us change over time with repeated obedience to God's Word marked by instances where we lapse.

God commands us to bear with one another in love. This means we expect that even if someone responds enthusiastically to a hard conversation, there may be work involved in change. We can validate and affirm forward growth while displaying patience and forgiveness during stumbles.

Sometimes we may be the ideal person to have a hard conversation, and yet *not* be the ideal person to support them in the long run. This can be true if the area where the individual needs to change is one we've struggled with and have only recently overcome (as in addiction). We also need to be careful about committing to intensive support when romantic attraction may become a real or perceived factor. In these instances, our plan should be to facilitate a connection with someone who can support them down the road.

When hard conversations center around delivering bad news, we may be prepared to remain with a person to offer comfort or have phone numbers ready to call if the other person needs more support. Do we know whom the person can consult if the individual has questions regarding the news (a physician, a website, someone else who has experienced the same thing)?

If the bad news affects the person physically (perhaps an older individual or someone with health complications), are we prepared to call medical support? If the news could be traumatic (especially for a child or young person), do we have the contact information for a professional who can help assess that person's needs?

It can be useful to consider with the other person the potential consequences for not changing, acting, or accepting the hard conversation. This isn't about punishment or correction, but more about helping others think through how their lives affect themselves and the people around them. How does a short temper interfere with relationships? How does gossip affect the body of Christ? How might persistent unbelief affect an individual?

Realistically, we cannot always have all of this figured out, but just asking ourselves the question as we prepare can open our minds to possible options. Remember that as hopeful believers, we prepare for success.

ARTwork

Answer: What support has been helpful for you in making important changes? How can you use that experience to help someone else?

Read: What are the instructions and the cautions in Galatians 6:1–10 for bearing with one another?

Try: Look down the road. People are responsible for their actions. While we may be responsible for telling them the truth, change is up to them. When I'm talking with others and they suggest they don't want to change, I affirm their freedom to make their own choices, but then I ask them the following question: "What does it look like down the road if you continue in this behavior?" A month from now? One year from now? Five years? What does it look like for you and for others? This single question can guide people into a greater view of the consequences of their actions.

Lesson 2

Biblical Boundaries

And Jonathan told David, "Saul my father seeks to
kill you. Therefore be on your guard in the morning.
Stay in a secret place and hide yourself."
(1 Sam. 19:2)

Plan B (for boundaries) is what we may do if our words are rejected. If someone's poor choices are causing harm to us, him- or herself, or others, we may need to establish firm boundaries around future interaction. These are often the hardest conversations of all.

In navigating situations like this in my own life, I've always found the story of David and Saul to be instructive. In 1 Samuel 18:10–11, we read, "The next day a harmful spirit from God rushed upon Saul, and he raved within his house while David was playing the lyre, as he did day by day. Saul had his spear in his hand. And Saul hurled the spear, for he thought, 'I will pin David to the wall.' But David evaded him twice."

Saul had loved David once but became a danger to him. It required David to put distance between himself and Saul. However, we watch David continue to treat Saul with respect and insist that others do, too (albeit from a distance). Loving, biblical boundaries protect us from flying spears.

Loving, biblical boundaries protect us from flying spears.

I've had to sit in numerous households discussing the impact of harmful choices and the real threat of separation from loved ones. It's best to be gentle but clear about the available choices. For example:

> Her: But I want to stay with their father. I know he hurts me, but he's always sorry later.

> Me: You're an adult, and no one can stop you from being with him, if that's your choice. However, you can't make the choice to allow your children to witness violence and expect others to stand by and not act. If you won't protect your children, others will.

Or:

> Him: What you and I talk about is confidential, right? You can't go around telling other people what I say.

> Me: Confidentiality has limits. I'll keep your matters private, unless what I learn is that you plan to harm yourself or others. Then I'd have to involve other people in our discussion.

Or:

> Her: I have a right to have a few beers. I'm a grown-up. No one can stop me from tossing back a few after a hard day.

Me: True, but your children also have rights. They have the right to be cared for by a sober adult, capable of making clearheaded decisions. If you're under the influence while being their sole caregiver, others have the right to remove them from your care.

Knowing our plan going into a hard conversation helps us remain calm and clearheaded (most of the time). If the people in our conversations choose to make positive choices, we'll know what help is available. If they make other choices, we've stated clearly what they're facing, so no one is surprised later.

These are important questions to consider even when our hard conversation is with a passing stranger. Will we invite the stranger to our church? Will we offer to pray for him or her? (And if we do offer, we should make good on our word.) Will we exchange phone numbers or emails with this individual and offer to have more conversations? Safety, location, personal boundaries, gender, age, and social context all play parts in these decisions.

If the conversation we're having is with someone we know, are we willing to have follow-up chats? Are we able to invest further in the lives of those around us if they require support to change? If we confront them with the gospel and they choose Christ, are we willing to be part of their spiritual journey going forward?

An initial hard conversation is a doorway to a deeper relationship.

There's no right answer here. Sometimes it's impractical to say yes. A young married man may confront a woman on her rude behavior at work only to discover she's depressed and struggling to keep food on the table for her children after their father left her. It probably wouldn't make sense for him to start showing up at her house alone with money for rent and food, but he could connect her with his church, or together, he and his wife may agree to provide practical support.

If the hard conversation is a difference of theology or biblical application with another believer, is it an issue over which you might part ways or something on which you're willing to agree to disagree? Stating this at the beginning helps everyone either relax, knowing they'll emerge on the other side, or pay attention because a relationship is at stake.

Other times, an initial hard conversation is a doorway to a deeper relationship, and we must be willing to provide ongoing encouragement, further conversation, or even practical support such as a ride to rehab, a warm meal, a listening ear, or discipleship. Too often, Christians have been guilty of delivering hard-hitting conversations without a willingness to develop a deeper relationship with the recipients of their "drive-by truthings." We can do better, in Jesus's name.

Of course, when we engage in hard conversations with people over the Internet, we must ask the same question, but it's more likely to involve how long we'll dialogue with a stranger, or how intensely we're willing to explore a difference of opinion in front of an online audience.

Jesus always remembered (and so should we) that in most conversations, there are participants and spectators. Those listening in or looking on may be just as affected as the key people engaged in dialogue. Wisdom always takes this into consideration.

ARTwork

Answer: When has someone walked with you through a difficult time in a way that truly helped? What did that support look like?

Read: In 1 Samuel 24, read how David treated Saul even as Saul pursued David's life. How is this a good example of how to set a firm boundary around someone's bad behavior while still respecting that person as an individual?

Try: If you find yourself in a surprise confrontation, employ the PSALM strategy.

1. Palm pause: Hold up your hand and interrupt the conversation. "I'm sorry. I need us to pause."
2. State the obvious: "I'm uncomfortable continuing at this moment, now that I understand the nature of our conversation, but I do care what you have to say."

3. Act on your words: Gather your things or stand to underline your intention.
4. Leave with a plan: "Let's plan to pick this up when I'm better prepared. Are you available on X?"
5. Minimize potential escalation: Assure the person you want to be open to him or her and to God when you meet again. Ask that neither of you discuss it with others until then and agree you'll both pray for a fruitful follow-up conversation. Key to maximizing the effectiveness of this strategy is to keep your end of the agreement by discussing it only with God and showing up for the second conversation with an open heart, not a ready defense.

Lesson 3

Hard Stops for Hard Conversations

And the king returned from the palace garden to the place where they were drinking wine, as Haman was falling on the couch where Esther was. And the king said, "Will he even assault the queen in my presence, in my own house?" As the word left the mouth of the king, they covered Haman's face. (Esther 7:8)

If anyone in the conversation expresses thoughts of self-harm or threats of violence to others, it's time to halt all and address that.

This means involving professionals, either law enforcement or medical/mental health first responders, to complete an adequate assessment. If you're a professional, you've been trained in this. If you're not, feel free to use words along these lines: "It's not my practice to ignore statements of such a serious nature. What I hear you saying is that you've had thoughts of taking your own life—or you're thinking about physically harming someone. Since I'm not trained to assess that thinking, I need to invite someone who is to join our conversation." You can explain who that might be—911, your ministry leader, the safety officer on your job, or local first responders' nonemergency line. "We can reach out to those people together, but if you're not willing to do that, please understand that I will have to contact someone for you."

> **If anyone in the conversation expresses thoughts of self-harm or threats of violence to others, it's time to halt all and address that.**

If you're the person having the thoughts, the process is the same. We can be in an intense conversation when we suddenly realize we need help or support (this can be especially true in hard conversations with our own loved ones). There's no shame in that. Sometimes another person's crisis brings our old memories to the surface or we become overwhelmed when a loved one chooses destructive ways. Managing everyone's feelings at once can diminish our conversational skills. End the conversation. Seek a trusted professional for evaluation.

If anyone makes statements that lead us to suspect a child (anyone under eighteen) is at risk of neglect or abuse, we have a moral duty and a legal responsibility to report our suspicion to child protective authorities.

If it's a child or young person disclosing abuse to you, express belief, assure that person it was right to speak out, and calmly explain that you will have to bring another person or people (helping people with special training in protecting children/youth) into your conversation. (Check with your state for specific guidelines and avenues for reporting. In many states, this can be done anonymously, if you have any fears for your own safety, or if the person is close to you.)

It's also important to report to child protective authorities if we have reason to suspect children are present during a situation of domestic violence. Witnessing domestic violence (including hearing it) can wreak serious harm on children.

When having conversations with people who've wrestled with addiction of any kind, it's helpful to acknowledge that you're aware that deception is frequently a symptom of addiction. Let the other people know that if you question their statements, you aren't calling them a liar, but acknowledging they may lie about this one thing, just as every person wrestling with addiction sometimes does. For example, you might calmly say, "I'm going to question the truth of that statement and give you the opportunity to correct yourself. I want to be sure it's you speaking and not the addiction."

If you have questions about this section, reach out to local authorities in law enforcement, human/social services, or your church staff for further explanation about laws in your state, policies governing your group, and useful approaches with specific populations.

ARTwork

Answer: When someone discloses abuse or thoughts of harm, what are the possible consequences of not taking that person seriously?

Read: In Acts 9:23–31, twice Saul's life is threatened. Who comes to his rescue and what does this rescue entail?

Try: Research the laws of your state; the policies of your workplace, ministry, or church; and local resources for reporting or helping with the topics introduced in this lesson. Store them in a readily accessible location.

HEART OF THE ART PRACTICE

Consider the great cloud of witnesses mentioned in Hebrews 12. What do they witness in your life as evidence that you love the person with whom you want to have a hard conversation? What can you do this week to provide them with more evidence that you are growing in love?

PART 3

Putting the Art into Practice

UNIT 12

Openings and Agreements

Lesson 1

Perfect Opening Line

*But one thing I do: forgetting what lies behind
and straining forward to what lies ahead, I press
on toward the goal for the prize of the upward
call of God in Christ Jesus. (Phil. 3:13–14)*

I stared at the blank page of this chapter far too long before I remembered a key principle of productive writing. Don't worry about creating the perfect beginning. There's greater value in getting words on the page than in having the perfect opening line. It's always possible to go back and rework the opening once you've written what needs to be said.

Honestly, this principle also holds true for hard conversations. Too often, it's that opening line that hangs us up. We wait for the perfect words, moment, or opportunity that never quite presents itself. So many important truths remain unspoken due to this unnecessary stall.

Make a habit of asking God to provide opportunities for certain hard conversations. For example, ask for a recognizable teachable moment with an adult child. Pray for confirmation you're the right person to have a hard chat with a fellow Christian by finding yourselves alone with sufficient time. God often provides, but truly, we live in the real and rocky world. Hard conversations often arise after an imperfect opening.

Certainly, bad first impressions can be hard to overcome, and rocky openings present a challenge. As Christians, though, we know faulty starts aren't necessarily the last word on anything. God is the redeemer who enters in to reclaim our stories when we've botched our beginnings. Model this in hard conversations.

Hard conversations often arise after an imperfect opening.

Delia frustrated me to no end. A hallmark of crisis meetings I facilitate is that we begin with a celebration of what is going well. I love this ritual and most participants come to love it too.

Not Delia. Delia was so unfamiliar and uncomfortable with success, she single-handedly hijacked our first few meetings. Before I could initiate introductions, Delia launched into a litany of complaints about her teenager, each presented as an insurmountable crisis. The teen would then dash from the room either in rage or embarrassment and Delia would wave a hand, declaring, "You see? That's what I'm dealing with!"

I tried explaining the process before the meeting. I tried racing Delia to the opening with no success (she was fast). I tried a giant self-adhesive note with our agenda and CELEBRATION listed at the top. All to no avail.

Then I remembered I follow Jesus. If I couldn't start the meeting perfectly, perhaps I could redeem it.

Rocky starts can be redeemed.

Instead of trying to beat Delia to the punch, I relaxed and remained quiet as she launched her usual negativity. I held a hand up to signal the teen to hold on. Once Delia paused for breath, I placed a hand on her elbow and spoke quietly. "That does sound important to discuss. Before we do, I'm going to insist that everyone state one thing that went well this week. We'll start with Aunt Tanya and we'll end back here with you, so we can pick right up on what you're saying, Delia. Tanya, what went well this week?"

God continually reminds me rocky starts can be redeemed.

Even with all our prayers and planning, hard conversations can occur before we can start them the way we'd hoped. It's that volcanic brew of emotion pressurized by procrastination that creates more of an eruption than an emerging. As Christians, we know all is not lost simply because of an imperfect beginning.

My best counsel on starting a hard conversation is to be transparent about your intentions. As in "Dad, I'd like an opportunity to talk with you about something of a spiritual nature. Could we meet for dinner?" or "Molly, I'm struggling with some aspects of your leadership style. I'm wondering if you have time for us to talk it through right now, or if we should schedule an appointment?" or "Kenya, I'm angry about what just happened. If we talk right now, I'll probably say things I don't mean, but you and I need to hash this out. What if we plan to take a walk in about an hour, after I've had time to cool off?"

> **The dawn of a discussion does not have to determine its destination.**

But sometimes we'll find ourselves in the middle of a hard conversation gone wrong. That's when we need to remember redemption and the power of Jesus Christ to intervene even after a poor start. The dawn of a discussion does not have to determine its destination.

If you find yourself dealing with an unfortunate opening, use body language to reinforce your words. Lean back, take a step away, hold up your hand, or make the time-out sign as you speak. It may sound like this.

"Wow, this is not how I wanted this conversation to go. This is too important to get lost in angry words or mean-spirited comments. I apologize for letting us get to this place. Can we take a breath and see if we can redeem the topic with calmer, clearer conversation?"

Or "I'm not thrilled with how we've arrived at this topic, but since we've landed on it, I have to admit I've wanted to discuss this. Still, I didn't plan to catch you off guard. Are you okay if we talk about it now, or should we take a break and reconvene when you've had time to prepare?"

Or "I'm going to stop us from continuing down this path until we move to a more private setting. What you're saying is too important not to merit my full attention, but I'm very conscious that others may overhear us."

Use your own wording, but the point is, we don't need to jump on every conversational bullet train and ride it to some dark tunnel ending. We can switch tracks, or at least make the attempt. The other person may be determined to continue at high speed, but even then, we can opt out by discontinuing the chat altogether.

If a hard conversation bursts out of the blue or if we botch our beginning, we remember that redemption is possible and then open the door for Jesus to do that work in the moment.

ARTwork

Answer: When have you experienced a relationship or situation that started off on the wrong foot, but then turned out well? What was the catalyst for the switch?

Read: Read Ruth 1 and then Ruth 4. Imagine Ruth's testimony at the end of the first chapter compared to the end of chapter 4.

Try: Recalculate. When a conversation gets out of hand, we can treat it just as if we'd gotten lost on a car ride. Pause. Remind everyone of the point and the goal. Review or add ground rules. Return to the last place you were before you got lost. Resume.

Lesson 2

Agree to Agree

All these with one accord were devoting themselves
to prayer, together with the women and Mary the
mother of Jesus, and his brothers. (Acts 1:14)

God demonstrated throughout the Old Testament the power of establishing markers at the places where people agree. The early church was born in prayer and agreement in an upper room in Jerusalem. We can live out this foundation of building on agreement in our conversations.

I was chatting with a dear friend when suddenly, our chat took a theological turn.

"I just don't get the Old Testament," she said. "It feels like it's a different God than Jesus. I don't know how anyone reconciles the things that happened in the Old Testament with our faith. I just focus on Jesus and ignore the rest."

Oh no. In the nanoseconds between her statement and my response, I flashed on all the ways our conversation could go wrong. I'm passionate about the Old Testament. I understand people's struggles with it, but I see a consistent God from Genesis through Revelation. It horrifies me when people exclude one testament from their spiritual education.

But from the tone of her voice and the passion of her statement, I worried that if I said that, we'd find ourselves on opposite sides of a great divide. Love and truth, I reminded myself. So, I responded with the words of the previous paragraph. I even doubled down. "In fact, I see evidence of Jesus throughout all of Scripture."

"How can you say that?" she asked, her voice rising. "How can God have a favorite nation or destroy entire people groups just because they aren't His chosen people? Where is Jesus in that?"

My anxiety escalated. I'm no proponent of genocide (I don't believe God is either), but what if my response made it sound as if I am?

Conversations, like car trips, can benefit from detours and scenic overlooks.

Thankfully, I remembered I'm not trapped into one straight conversational track. Discussions don't have to proceed like speeding trains. Conversations, like car trips, can benefit from detours and scenic overlooks. So, like a GPS, I recalculated. "I do have thoughts on that, but before I launch into them, may I ask you a question?"

"Yes, of course."

"I've seen too many friendships destroyed over differences in theology.

Is there anything I could say in response to your question that would jeopardize our friendship?"

She laughed. "Of course not. I might disagree, but I know your heart for Jesus. People can have differences and continue to be close friends, can't they? I'm open to a discussion about this, and I'm really interested in your opinion. You're important to me."

Whew. "Thank you. I feel the same about you. Now, let me tell you my thoughts."

This brief departure from a place of controversy to a safe, stable landing reduced my stress a hundredfold. My friend and I proceeded to have an intense conversation with much disagreement, but we did so with reduced personal tension because we focused on not doing harm.

Many hard conversations arise around conflict or differences in either theology or worldview. Turtles see these conversations coming and run in the opposite directions. Hawks may welcome them but then find themselves caught in an ever-revolving door of discussion that never resolves, or worse, that silences the other person and discourages future conversations.

Starting from and then frequently revisiting places of agreement can maintain engagement in what may become heated talks. Any time in a hard conversation that we can find a place of agreement, we benefit from noting (even celebrating) that. It can be a great challenge to find this, so openly seeking it is key.

> **People seeking power exploit weakness; people seeking resolution build on strengths.**

Begin hard conversations with affirmations or celebrations of even small successes, as I described in my story about Delia. God knew the power of celebration, and we're wise to incorporate it whenever we can.

There are often more places of agreement than we realize, because we don't seek them. People seeking power exploit weakness; people seeking resolution build on strengths.

The psalmist says, "Blessed are those whose strength is in you, in whose heart are the highways to Zion. As they go through the Valley of

Baca they make it a place of springs; the early rain also covers it with pools. They go from strength to strength; each one appears before God in Zion" (Ps. 84:5–7).

ARTWORK

Answer: What simple ways can you find to celebrate or acknowledge points of agreement in your family, work, church, or community? What are ways to recognize others' strengths on an ongoing basis?

Read: In 1 Corinthians 1, Paul is exhorting the church at Corinth to find agreement rather than be divided. As you read this chapter, note all the places this church was likely in agreement. Do these seem like greater or lesser issues than those that divided them?

Try: Consider the person with whom you hope to have a hard conversation. List as many areas of agreement with that person as you can.

Lesson 3

Imperfect Agreement

> *Then Laban said to Jacob, "See this heap and the pillar, which I have set between you and me. This heap is a witness, and the pillar is a witness, that I will not pass over this heap to you, and you will not pass over this heap and this pillar to me, to do harm. The God of Abraham and the God of Nahor, the God of their father, judge between us." (Gen. 31:51–53)*

We don't even need people to agree on situational facts to find areas of agreement. That sounds contradictory, but here are a couple of examples:

> Mother: Sarah dawdles in her room, never has her stuff together, and misses the bus most days. That's why we're headed to truancy court.

Sarah: Mom won't let me have an alarm clock, and she never wakes us up on time. She'll promise to do laundry, but then doesn't, so I don't have the right clothes. Then she'll fight with me, so that I'm late. I'm tired of missing my first class and always being in trouble.

Me: Okay, even though we don't agree about why it's happening, it's good to see everyone agrees Sarah is frequently late for school. We agree it would be best for Sarah to get to the bus and her first class. And it sounds like we agree that both Mom and Sarah have something to do with making that happen. Yes? Going forward, what is something each of you can do differently?

With that one paragraph, we've moved the conversation from a dispute of the history of the problem to a place of shared vision for the future and teamwork to come up with a corrective plan.

Or what about a husband and wife in a hard conversation about responsibilities?

Her: I'm tired of coming home from work to find you already playing video games and the house a mess with no sign of dinner started. Why do I have to be the grown-up all the time?

Him: I'm tired of the nagging and you complaining every time I play video games. I get home before you, and that feels like the only time I can play without you making me feel guilty.

Her: Well, it sounds like we can at least agree we're both tired. And I agree that I do try to make you feel guilty about gaming.

Him: Okay, I agree I don't clean anything or start thinking about supper until you walk through the door.

Her: Since we agree we're both tired, can we agree to schedule a conversation about this at lunch tomorrow? And can we agree that you'll stop playing the game long enough to help me clean up and make supper? After dinner, I won't make you feel guilty for playing until nine o'clock.

Couples can almost make a game or friendly competition of finding places of agreement in the middle of an argument. It sounds corny, but in practice, it's powerful.

When groups experience conflict, it can be unifying to stop discussing the dispute long enough to brainstorm what strengths your group has. Make a list of what you're doing right and display that list during every meeting.

You may choose to go a step further and ask the group to identify a strength of each person in the room. (An encouraging variation is to write everyone's name on an envelope. Pass the envelopes around and ask group members to write a strength they see in that individual on a square of paper and place it in the envelope.)

Keep these strength lists handy. The discussion leader can reference these lists, as in "How did we become so strong at fund-raising? Are there skills we used there that we can apply to solving this conflict?" or "Let's pause for a moment because we're all getting a little heated. Ricardo, we've agreed your strength is being a prayer warrior. Would you mind leading us in prayer?" or "Song-min, we've agreed you have an eye for detail. Are there things we've neglected to consider here?"

When conflict is particularly challenging, it can be helpful for Christians to remember we have a common enemy who wants to divide. Sometimes the only agreement we can find is that we don't want that enemy to win, but that can be enough to regain solid ground for conversation.

The more we make finding places of agreement or identifying strengths a habit, the more impact it will have on increasing the effectiveness of conversations. Young people will pick up on this habit if they see it often enough.

It feels awkward initially, so we must be diligent in reinforcing it until we have a history of seeing its value. In practice, it can be redemptive.

ARTWORK

Answer: Describe a friendship or relationship you've developed with someone with whom you have some areas of disagreement. How have you both benefited from the friendship?

Read: Genesis 31 describes an intense disagreement between Laban and Jacob. They don't resolve the details of their conflict, but they submit to God's desire for the two to part with a promise of peace. They establish a *mizpah*, a heap of stones signifying that God witnessed their agreement not to harm each other. Look for places within your hard conversations to "heap up agreements" like stones as reminders that God witnesses your conversation.

Try: Seek silent prayer. Christians know that prayer during conflict can be beneficial. However, we also know that in practice, people praying aloud in groups may use the airspace to preach or plead their side. It can make sense to pause for prayer, but I recommend a time of silent prayer—especially if there are only two of you. Simply agree on a time limit but keep your prayers private. This reduces the temptation to continue the argument under the guise of inviting God in.

HEART OF THE ART PRACTICE

When to Thump Your Bible

"Bible-thumping" is a derogatory term referring to anyone who aggressively promotes Christianity or quotes the Bible as an authority for his or her arguments. Reasonable Christians disagree about when it makes sense to introduce Scripture into a hard conversation, so I thought I'd weigh in with my thoughts. Take them for what they're worth.

With Opponents and Skeptics

My hawk side feels bombarded in these times by people who unapologetically expound on their passions, often quoting sources with whom I vehemently disagree or intellectually dismiss. My discomfort doesn't stop them from citing famous atheists, promoting political or spiritual views that are offensive to me, or making sweeping judgments about people who might reject their points of view.

This then motivates my hawk self to cite the Bible as an authoritative reference without apology and promote my worldview as passionately and unapologetically as they. I've found that forceful debaters respect direct rebuttal, and so, more often, in discussion with skeptics or opponents of the faith, I take a direct approach to argument.

I will generally acknowledge that they will likely not see biblical teaching as authoritative but remind them that I do come to the conversation from that perspective, so I will reference it as a source. I try to do this calmly and within the context of a conversation, not hurling Scripture about like we're in a boulder-tossing competition. (I only reference specific passages if they ask.)

My turtle side benefits in public conversations with people who oppose our faith from remembering that I'm not alone. So, in less forceful conversations (for example, in the workplace), I may not quote the Bible but will explain that my perspective is informed by ancient, historic, biblical teaching that has been respected by great minds for centuries. When asked why I've taken a position or chosen a specific practice, I simply state that my study of the Bible informs most of my life philosophy and offer to go into detail if the other person is interested in hearing more. Sometimes that happens.

With Christians

In hard conversations with other believers, I believe it's kind to be circumspect about quoting God's Word.

When the hard conversation is of a theological nature or is a disagreement about a certain practice, it's wise to ask questions before engaging in a scriptural duel, which sounds like this.

"Well, what do you have to say about this verse?"

"Oh yeah, well, I'll see you this verse and raise you this verse."

This is not the healthiest or most honorable use of God's Word. Instead, ask questions similar to the following.

"What's your understanding of the Bible's teaching on your position?"

Or "That's a different application of that passage than I'm accustomed to hearing. Can you tell me more about how that fits in with your understanding of other passages that teach what I'm saying?"

Employ the other tools I've described in the ARTwork and Heart of the Art Practice sections. Exercise humility and restraint. Use caution when debating a brother or sister in Christ.

It's good practice to review Romans 14 and 15 often. Using caution and gentleness is not the same as dismissing our own understanding of Scripture or implying that it doesn't matter what position one takes on a theological issue. It is simply to say that brothers and sisters must disagree within the guidelines established by our Father, who rules.

Consider 2 Timothy 2:23–26: "Have nothing to do with foolish, ignorant controversies; you know that they breed quarrels. And the Lord's servant must not be quarrelsome but kind to everyone, able to teach, patiently enduring evil, correcting his opponents with gentleness. God may perhaps grant them repentance leading to a knowledge of the truth, and they may come to their senses and escape from the snare of the devil, after being captured by him to do his will."

In a hard conversation involving correction among believers, gentleness, again, should reign. Certainly, reference Bible verses and passages, but do so in an instructive manner, not wielding them like billy clubs. Consider Galatians 6:1: "Brothers, if anyone is caught in any transgression, you who are spiritual should restore him in a spirit of gentleness. Keep watch on yourself, lest you too be tempted."

When comforting others with God's Word in times of trial, disaster, disease, or death, do ensure you're using Bible verses properly and that they are actual Bible verses. Discuss your counsel with your pastor or Bible teacher.

And this. Please let me emphasize this. Spend as much time considering how to encourage others with God's Word as you do considering how to correct them with it. Making this a habit will earn you credibility for times when you're referencing Scripture during confrontation or correction.

Now We're Talking
(Tips for Midtalk)

Lesson 1

The Only Gotcha

We who are strong have an obligation to bear with the failings of the weak, and not to please ourselves. Let each of us please his neighbor for his good, to build him up. (Rom. 15:1–2)

I was doing something I shouldn't.

In my early twenties, I rebelled. That's not a decade to tire of obeying Jesus. The consequences are too high. Thankfully, I had friends who weren't afraid to engage in hard conversations, and they knew what to do when I avoided them.

It was late at night when I left the apartment of the wrong person. As I rounded the block to my car, I spied two of my church friends, Victor and Pam, leaning against my red Ford Tempo.

"What are you guys doing out here?" I asked, trying to sound nonchalant.

"We're here to take you for coffee, and we're not going to stop talking until you remember who you are."

I remember the icy cold in my veins and my racing heart, realizing I hadn't fooled anyone. "What do you mean?"

"This isn't the life you're meant to live. Don't pretend with us. We're
worried about you and now, we're all going to talk."

And we did.

It wasn't easy. We drank a lot of coffee. I cried and talked. They listened. They didn't preach, but they also didn't let me get away with lame
excuses or justifications. By dawn, I had a plan for repentance, and they
had a plan for keeping me accountable.

It doesn't always go that way, but it could go that way more often if
we tried. The horror of being confronted in wrongdoing was real, but
my lasting memory is how loved I felt. I had friends who were willing
to track me down, wait for me in the dark, and stay up all night to hear
me out.

> **The only gotcha in a hard conversation with a
> Christian should be "I've *gotcha* best interests in
> mind."**

And not once did anyone say, "Ha! We suspected all along you
weren't a *real* Christian." In fact, what Victor kept saying quietly was,
"This is not who you are. You may have forgotten, but we haven't."
They demonstrated that the only gotcha in a hard conversation with a
Christian should be "I've *gotcha* best interests in mind."

They didn't toss Bible verses like mini grenades, but I occasionally
did—misusing them to justify myself. Whenever I dared this, though,
Pam would respond, "Do you really need me to re-explain that passage to you?" or "Do you need me to counter that verse with another?
Because I imagine God's already brought an answering passage to your
mind." And God had.

Repeatedly, they assured me that if I wasn't valuable to them, they
wouldn't be there in the middle of the night having that conversation
with me. They could be this amazing, not because they were perfect
Christians, but because they, too, knew who they were in Jesus. They
spoke gently because they knew they, too, were susceptible to temptations. They were steadfast because they, too, knew the truth of God's
Word.

ARTWORK

Answer: When has someone been patient with you in weakness? How did the person demonstrate that patience?

Read: Romans 14 and 15 offer strong guidelines for Christians who have some areas of difference. List some of these in your own words.

Try: It's time. Remember that hard conversation that inspired you to read this book? Work through the six questions in preparation.

Lesson 2

Slowly I Turned

There is one whose rash words are like sword thrusts,
but the tongue of the wise brings healing.
(Prov. 12:18)

There's an old vaudeville bit made famous to my generation by the Three Stooges, Abbott and Costello, and Lucille Ball. The main character is triggered to anger by a specific word or phrase. She acts just fine until someone says that word. Then, saying, "Slowly, I turned, step by step," she transforms into an aggressor against the one who inadvertently triggered her.

If we aren't careful, a version of this sketch can happen in hard conversations. We wander in and accidentally say or do something that triggers the other person's fight-or-flight instinct. With a little bit of planning, these triggers are easy to avoid and give our conversations a greater chance of success.

First, let's discuss words to avoid. It should go without repeating that as Christians, we need to cleanse our conversations of cursing, coarse language, offensive references, and racial slurs. Sometimes, in anger and in emotionally intense situations, these kinds of words erupt. It's unfortunate, but life gets real, quickly sometimes.

If this is uncharacteristic of the person or people in the conversation, it's usually a signal to pause and allow everyone the opportunity to regain self-control. Intense conversations don't bring the best out in some of us. Offer a short break and the opportunity to apologize upon returning to the conversation. Remind everyone that we're all in process and that risk of exposing that process is not a reason to give up talking together.

If we're the offender, the best corrective action is to immediately take responsibility, apologize, repent, and discontinue the conversation if need be, until we have a better emotional or spiritual handle. This may be only a few minutes, but it may mean tabling the conversation for another time.

If we're in conversation with someone for whom this type of language or behavior is characteristic (a coworker, rebellious teen, unsaved family member, or a person to whom we're reaching out), we may choose to set boundaries around the behavior, end the conversation, or "planned ignore," depending on the spiritual state of the person and the goal of the conversation.

▌ Life gets real, quickly sometimes.

If we're going to choose to set boundaries or "planned ignore" and there are others present, we should briefly explain what we're doing: "Tom, I'm not a fan of that kind of language, but I'm more concerned with hearing you than correcting you. So, if it's all right with Ed, I won't put the brakes on our conversation because of a few bad words. If you're not directing them at anyone, we'll keep talking. Okay with you, Ed?"

Or "We have two diverse groups in the room, and our goal is to work through an important disagreement. During that time, people may use language that others find unpleasant to hear. Can we all agree that for the next hour, we'll focus on what each person is saying and not on the specific words he or she is using? We will address destructive language, but let's do it once we've built a foundation of agreement."

Next, let's look at some words and phrases that aren't necessarily a sin issue but are still more inflammatory than useful in hard conversations. These include words like *never* and *always*, as in "You always show up late" or "You never follow through with your promises." When those phrases appear, ask questions that make them disappear, such as "Wow, always is a lot. Give me an example. How many times was Shiloh late this past week?" or "Nguyen always ignores what you're saying? Give me an example of how that played out yesterday."

▌ Eliminate words that involve phantom people.

Eliminate words that involve phantom people, as in "Everyone agrees the pastor is boring" or "Several people have registered complaints about the Sunday school." These too can be teased out by asking specifics: "That's important for us to follow up. Can you give us the names of two or three?"

Accusatory phrases or phrases that imply the other person is either foolish or less intelligent are important to eliminate: "How can you even think that?" or "Who in their right mind believes something like that?" or "How can you believe that and call yourself a Christian?" More productive approaches include "Help me understand your thinking on this subject" or "I'm curious to know the factors that led up to you making that choice."

Next, let's talk about using organic humor but avoiding sarcasm. Many people, including myself, use humor to diffuse tense situations. It's extremely useful, but we must exercise caution. We don't want others to think we're laughing at them or making light of their pain, so we only inject humor when we're certain of our audience. Also, sarcasm is rarely helpful in hard conversations and is more likely to create hurt than healing, so it's best to leave that for lighter times.

Although, when people use sarcasm to express deep pain, it can shut down conversation to insist they change their tone (especially with teens). Set a kind boundary by acknowledging the sarcasm as a tool, while encouraging them to explore other ways of speaking. For example: "It's understandable that you're using sarcasm right now to express some deep emotions, but I want you to know you're safe talking with me about this, even if you choose to drop the sarcasm as a defense."

It is wise to allow others to use humor or to laugh even in dark situations. For many people, this is an important coping mechanism. Individuals in high-stress jobs such as military personnel, first responders, mental health or medical professionals, and people who have endured intense suffering often develop a language around humor that may seem a bit morbid to outsiders. This is a powerful strategy for filtering feelings about what they've experienced without falling apart.

| **It is wise to allow others to use humor or to laugh even in dark situations.**

Finally, it's useful for the family of God to use words everyone understands. Sometimes we think we're speaking the same language only to find we're not. If an American goes to England and orders chips with a meal, it can be disconcerting to receive French fries instead of the anticipated salty snack food.

We Christians have words that are unique to our faith, many of which are important to specifically define (such as redemption, atonement, or Communion), while others have meanings that can vary from person to person (such as blessing, worship, or ministry). It's wise to ask people what they mean when they say, for instance, "I truly worshipped today" or "I'm praying to receive a blessing" or "I feel as if I don't have any opportunity for ministry."

I was in a meeting in which people were debating the merits of a church's contemporary service versus the traditional service. A church leader who attended both services kept repeating, "I really sense the Holy Spirit moving during the contemporary service."

I could see this visibly discouraging those from the traditional service. I realized I didn't know what she meant, so I asked, "How do you see the Holy Spirit move during the contemporary service? Why do you suppose the Holy Spirit likes that service better?"

She stopped and thought. "Hmm. I don't think I meant to imply that. I guess what I mean is that with so little time to coordinate the music, the message, and other elements of that service, it must be the Holy Spirit who brings them together every week."

Another leader reflected, "But there isn't as much to coordinate in the traditional service since it follows a similar order each week. How do you know the Holy Spirit isn't just as active there?"

The first leader chuckled. "I guess I don't. That's something for me to think about next week. I'll pay more attention to looking for the Holy Spirit's work in that service."

It's simple enough to say to someone, "I think I know what you mean when you say that, but could you elaborate so I'm sure?" As we practice this, it's sure to lead to others asking about words or phrases they have misunderstood, perhaps for years.

We all have pet words or phrases we overuse. Sometimes we use them so often, they become an annoyance to others or virtually meaningless. Ask the people closest to you what your pet words or phrases are and what they think you mean when you say them.

ARTwork

Answer: What words or phrases do you use frequently? What do you suppose others think those words mean?

Read: Proverbs 18 is ripe with wisdom about engaging in conversation. Choose several verses to commit to memory.

Try: Only apologize for your own actions. Many hard conversations run off the rails, not at the first sign of trouble, but when we apologize for other people's actions. It sounds like this.

"I'm sorry you're offended."

"I apologize that your feelings are hurt."

"I'm sorry you're misunderstanding what I'm saying."

These are accusations and defenses disguised as apologies. Christians are above this. Remember our guardrails of truth and love. We should be experts at repentance, so when we do it, it should be recognizable as such. Truthful apologies sound like this.

"I've offended you and I'm sorry. That wasn't my intent, but I can see now how my words would cause offense."

"I've hurt you. I sincerely apologize. I hope you'll forgive me. How can I create a path for that?"

"I'm not being clear in expressing myself. Would you be willing to allow me to clear up the misunderstanding I've created?"

If you honestly don't believe you've done anything wrong, the solution is simple. Don't apologize. That's a toe dip into dishonesty. Acknowledge the situation in a more honest fashion.

"I can see you feel offended. That's not what my goal was here, but I stand by my words. Is there some way we can talk through why you've taken offense at them?"

"Am I right in that you're feeling hurt by what I've said? Is there anything I can say to move us toward healing?"

"I feel as though you're not understanding me. Maybe the emotions of our conversation are making it hard to do that and we'd benefit from taking a break until we're calmer."

Apologize for your own actions only; acknowledge your observation of the actions of others.

Lesson 3

Work-Arounds

Two are better than one, because they have
a good reward for their toil. (Eccl. 4:9)

Sometimes initial hard conversations are unsuccessful, unproductive, or downright explosive, but we want to try again. Other times, there are special circumstances that merit a different approach to having a talk, such as distance between parties, hearing challenges, or memory issues. Two useful strategies to employ in unusual situations are using writing during hard conversations and inviting in a third party.

Sometimes we might avoid conversations because we get emotional when we say the words aloud. Writing can be a wonderful way to share positive or loving thoughts.

Writing is also a beautiful way to clarify how a person can choose to follow Jesus or to offer assurances to an older person experiencing fears about death. Having the truth of salvation, along with appropriate Bible verses, written down can be a comforting reference for people prone to forgetfulness or fear. They can pull out what you've written whenever the concern returns.

I've done this for my father. Over the years, I know he's heard the gospel message from either myself or others, and at times it appeared he understood it. Even after he made a commitment to Christ, he would sometimes talk about guilt and fear of life after death. I wrote him a letter that clearly explained his salvation, God's forgiveness, and the reasons he doesn't have to fear death. He keeps the letter in his desk. I don't know how often he reads it, but the words are there for him whenever he needs them.

Writing is a powerful way to encourage someone who's going through hardship. Sending cards or notes with a few kind words and Bible references can be just the lifeline needed to hold on. Consider writing a verse a day on a calendar specifically for that person facing hardship, trial, or grief.

If we're having trouble getting someone to meet with us to discuss a conflict, if there's distance between us, or if we've tried face-to-face conversations with no success, writing can be helpful, but then we must factor in the risk. Anything written can still be misinterpreted, shared with other parties, or saved and used against us by quarrelsome people. If we must write part of a hard conversation, keep it brief. Be honest. Proceed with extreme caution. If it doesn't relate to a specific sin issue, have a mature friend read it for clarity, without explanation from you, and make suggested adjustments.

There are all kinds of hard conversations that are not about sin. For many of these, it's useful and wise to invite a third party for support. Delivering bad news or visiting someone who is suffering, grieving, or undergoing a trial can be less intimidating if we invite another friend along for support. Sometimes we've worked up our courage to share some deep truth about ourselves or to explain an important change in our lives (such as conversion to Christ, engaging in foreign missions, or leaving a lucrative job to enter the ministry) to a loved one, but we're afraid we'll lose our nerve. Again, bringing a supportive, mature friend can be a blessing both to us and to the others involved.

In matters of sin, the Bible is clear that a third party is only to be incorporated in the process once we've gone to our brother and sister in private and given them an opportunity to repent. Matthew 18:15–20 describes this process. Following it eliminates much trouble among believers.

There are disagreements about all kinds of issues that aren't about sin. Young couples may invite a more experienced couple to help them have a conversation about managing their finances or parenting. People from different cultures may gather with an experienced facilitator to try to understand one another better and educate one another about bridging differences.

When we're learning how to have hard conversations, we may invite a ministry partner or coworker to observe us and offer constructive feedback. Family members can invite other family members to sit in on conversations with a senior about his driving, with a teen about his behavior, or with children about the health of a parent. There are also numerous professionals available from clergy to social workers, medical professionals to mediators to therapists, we can include when appropriate.

ARTWORK

Answer: Do you save cards, notes, or emails others write to you? What makes them worth saving?

Read: Read Ecclesiastes 4:9–12 and Matthew 18:15–20. In your own words, explain when it's important to speak privately with someone and list times when it might be perfectly acceptable to bring along a friend for support.

Try: Team up. God had a wonderful idea when He included us in the family of God once we became followers of Jesus. Partner with another believer willing to learn how to have hard conversations and practice the skills in this book. First, practice with one another. Next, agree to observe one another using them in conversation and offer feedback. Start with conversations that are hard, but not conflict-based, such as visiting people in hospitals or convalescence homes or sharing stories about your relationship with God to your small group or with unbelieving friends.

Lesson 4

Stick the Landing

For I am already being poured out as a drink
offering, and the time of my departure has come.
I have fought the good fight, I have finished the
race, I have kept the faith. (2 Tim. 4:6–7)

I'd dreaded this moment, even though I knew it was inevitable. This lovely group of Christians were reading my first book and, from all reports, enjoying it. So much so, they'd invited me for conversation at a local coffeehouse near their church. This church, I knew, had different views than I do on some controversial issues.

The invitation had been extended months earlier, but now, an unsettling message popped up in my email. The group leader bravely bared her soul. "I love your writing, and I read your blog all the time. I want you to come chat with us, but I can tell you probably don't share our views on some matters. I'm afraid when you realize that, you won't want to come. Plus, some of our people are worried when they meet you, they won't like you, even though they love your writing. What should I do?"

This was a problem. Still, I adored the straightforward nature of that email. If only all of us could communicate so directly.

The simple thing would be to avoid the situation. Discussing debatable subjects in the church is my least favorite pastime (okay, cleaning out the sink strainer is my least favorite, but this is a close second). I could simply find some excuse to bow out and let us all off the hook. She and I briefly entertained that option but then chose to proceed in faith that God knew what He was doing.

It was a cozy group, and we got our coffee before finding seats. After my introduction, I invited questions. Immediately, a gentleman raised his hand. "I think you're a lot more conservative than we are. Some of us are worried about that and wondered if we should talk about it."

I admired this guy. What bravery! How could one not love this group that included at least two people willing to introduce a hard topic. I'd prayed about this. I'd talked it over with other Christian authors who speak. Then I'd prepared my reply that went something like this.

"Well, together we can decide how to proceed. We do have theological differences in some key areas. Let's consider our choices.

"You've read an entire book I've written about Jesus and faith. From what I understand, it had meaning for you. There's much in there on which we agree, so we could spend our time discussing that.

"I'm also willing to discuss areas where we disagree, with this understanding. I study to understand controversial areas of theology and work hard to determine what I think. Because of that, I don't apologize for what I believe. I'm not arrogant enough to imagine I've figured everything out perfectly, but I clearly consider my position right. If I didn't, I'd believe something else.

"By implication, I therefore have concluded a different position is faulted. That doesn't mean I think people who hold it are bad Christians. It simply means that on that point, we disagree, as believers have through the ages.

"If you've come to your conclusions through study of God's Word and have a different understanding of it than I do, I respect your process and would love to understand it more. If, however, you've come to your conclusions because you don't like (or don't know) what God's Word says and think it's outdated or needs to be changed, well then, you and I might have more of a problem reaching an understanding. We could still talk, but that conversation would center more on our view of God's Word.

"Either way, we start out tonight knowing we have many places of agreement centered on Jesus. The choice is yours. Shall we discuss the book or other topics?"

The group chose to discuss the book during that meeting, but I let them know the door was open to debate the more sensitive issues any time. Since then, I've had several one-on-one conversations with some of them about the controversies. While rigorous, those conversations haven't become adversarial, and we've all grown up a little having them.

One key to hard conversations is to stick the landing. That means no matter how smooth or rocky the beginning and middle have gone, find a way to end well. Martha didn't cut Jesus out of her life when He called her out on her attitude about Mary. In fact, they were still friends engaged in hard conversations when her brother Lazarus died.

Peter didn't walk away from Jesus when the Lord scolded him for having little faith or told him, "Get behind me, Satan," and Jesus didn't abandon Peter when Peter denied knowing Jesus. They continued to have hard conversations and Peter grew in faith.

> ### A Christian ending, even to a hard conversation, is rational and redemptive.

For those closest to Jesus, life was clearly a series of hard conversations. I've found this to be true every time I read my Bible and wrestle with the Lord in prayer. A Christian ending, even to a hard conversation, is rational and redemptive.

Sticking the landing might very well require persistence. Keep at it. Don't let one (or six) botched or rocky discussion(s) deter you from initiating more. Remember, the children of Israel marched around the walls of Jericho seven times before they fell.

I've worked with countless individuals or families who decided to discontinue a program or conversation that would help them get closer to their goals. Each time, I tried to end with what I call a redemptive summary. This is applauding what went well, acknowledging what still needs work, and leaving the door of hope open for Jesus to work.

As in "I'm sorry you've decided to stop working on this, but I respect your freedom to make this choice. I care about you, and particularly appreciate X, X, and X (X being strengths or positive qualities). It's normal for change to be a process, and it sometimes takes many stops and starts. If you ever want to pick up the conversation again, this is how to reach me."

Or "This conversation went as badly as I feared it would, but I believe God isn't finished. If you're willing, I'd love for us to try again. Can we plan to meet in one week? Is there someplace we could start where we agree—even if it's a small agreement? Can you think of someone to invite to be with us who might help us communicate more smoothly?"

Or "You've been clear you're not interested in following Jesus. I hope you know it's out of respect and love for you that I will always hope you change your mind. I'm not interested in hounding you, but would you mind if I pray for you? Would you be willing for me to bring the subject up again in three months? Six months?"

With groups or committees, we can make it part of each meeting to open by celebrating what's going right and conclude with a redemptive summary.

By now, I believe we can agree that hard conversations are an art that requires training, practice, and persistence. The ability to improve our skills in this art becomes more and more apparent in these times when it can feel frightening or even dangerous to disagree. The headlines are full of incidents that ignited because people didn't understand each other.

Jesus, however, modeled how to have hard conversations, tell the truth, engage people with opposing worldviews, and communicate love. The more we draw near to Him and study His ways, the better we'll be at viewing these conversations as ministries in which to be engaged, rather than battles to be fought and won.

We don't "win," biblically, by either convincing others of our views or shutting them down. Certainly, if we love others, we're going to try to persuade them of the gospel or a specific theological perspective, but our interest should be, primarily, their souls—not our own entertainment, sport, or need to be right.

In biblical terms, we "win" if we model Jesus's example of speaking truth and living love, even during a hard conversation (or by initiating one), even if no one is persuaded in that moment, even if no one cares that we're right.

ARTwork

Answer: What excites you most about learning how to have hard conversations?

Read: In John 13–17, Jesus speaks His last words to His disciples before His crucifixion. What can we learn from this about ending well in preparation for continuing the conversation?

Try: Park some concerns until later. Everyone operates under tight time constraints at times, and that can be a challenge when having a hard conversation, especially if the other person has much to discuss. One tool for navigating this is to ask permission to take notes while the other person (or people) identifies all their areas of concern. List the main topics. Then explain whatever time constraint you have and ask the other person to prioritize their concerns by urgency. Then, suggest that because time is short, you will discuss the top one or two topics at this meeting and schedule another to address the rest. This can demonstrate that you're taking all their concerns seriously and respecting their priorities, while still operating on a realistic timeline.

HEART OF THE ART PRACTICE

Hawks Uninterrupted

Making uninterrupted speeches is a valued skill when it's not happening inside a conversation. There are occasions and venues to exercise and develop this important ability. Finding an outlet for the depth of your passion on a topic can serve to "release the buildup of steam" we sometimes unleash on others.

Preaching, radio shows, podcasts, and public speaking are obvious avenues for this, but some hawks are finding they enjoy posting social media videos, either live or prerecorded, and they've developed a healthy following. Spoken-word poetry events are held in coffeehouses and clubs around the country. Research this medium and see if it may be for you.

Even if you're not interested in publishing videos for the wide world, your children may enjoy having a digitally recorded daily life-chat that you send via smartphone; or your congregation may like having a midweek word of encouragement by live chat. There is a time for everything, so seek out times to speak uninterrupted when others have the option to tune in.

Turtles May Ask Permission

When you're feeling hesitant about having a conversation, but it feels important to try, asking permission to speak about the topic can free you from your fear. It sounds a little like this.

"Hector, it sounds as if you're really struggling with getting your children to sleep at night. I've had some experience with that and have some ideas. Would you be open to me sharing them with you?"

"Miranda, I know you've been going through a lot lately, and I care about you. When I've faced hard times, my relationship with Jesus was the only thing that got me through. I'm happy to tell you about how it helped, if you're interested. Would you like to have coffee tomorrow?"

"Dear, I've been doing some reading about ways that Christian couples can manage their debt, and I'm excited about this one writer's ideas. Would you mind if I shared with you the ones I think apply to us, or would you be more comfortable reading the book and then discussing it with me?"

The other person may say no. But if you get a yes, then you can proceed knowing that person is aware of the topic and willing to let you at least begin a conversation.

UNIT 14

Commence Conversations

Lesson 1

No Guarantee

I have said these things to you, that in me you may
have peace. In the world you will have tribulation.
But take heart; I have overcome the world.
(John 16:33)

The young woman I was mentoring sat across from me, frustrated at
my suggestion. She crossed her arms and insisted she wasn't ready to
go solo.

"We've studied this, discussed it, and you've listened in while I've
had some hard conversations. Now, it's time for you to practice it with
your friend."

"But I'm not like you," she protested. "I won't do it right."

"First of all, you don't have to be like me. You have to be like Jesus.
Second, no one does it 'right.' When it comes to having conversations,
we all just do our best. You can do that. Let's work through the six
questions together so you're prepared. Then schedule a time to meet
with your friend."

"You have so many strategies with people, though. I think I only remember two."

I smiled. "How do you think I developed those strategies? I tried. I
failed. I tried again. If you only remember two strategies, remember that

Jesus only needed five loaves of bread and two fish to feed a multitude. He'll build on your two conversational tools."

Three days later, she arrived on my doorstep, beaming. "I did it. I used some of the stuff we've talked about and I was just honest. The hard part was getting started, but once I did that, it was amazing. We haven't worked everything out yet, but it was a solid beginning. And I didn't even need you. I was just me."

Like my young friend, now it's your turn to put into practice what you've read and studied. It's time to do what we've been describing. (Cheers from the hawks, sighs from the turtles, and the chameleons withhold comment.)

We've discussed how our individual conversational styles impact conversations. We've learned about invisible walls and how to overcome them. We've done the heart-work and asked the questions we need to ask to prepare. We've practiced some strategies and chosen one or two we especially like. Now what?

We all have conversations to initiate, and the only thing I can guarantee is that there are no guarantees. That's right. Even with all the principles and skills I've described, we aren't guaranteed the outcomes we desire from every hard conversation.

We've increased our ability to do less damage and to give God more room to work, but there are still challenges ahead. Employing these tools, I have more positive outcomes than negative, but there are still discussions that are more akin to riding a spooked pony than to conversing. That, loved ones, is just life this side of glory.

> **Hard conversations are the bare pavement of life, the place where soft souls skid across hard truth and walk away with skinned knees and road rash.**

I apologize that my encouragement, this "pregame pep talk," won't be all that encouraging, but it will be true.

We live in a fallen world. We interact with broken, messy, sinful people. Even when we follow Jesus, we remain imperfect, capable of sin.

Hard conversations are the bare pavement of life, the place where soft souls skid across hard truth and walk away with skinned knees and road rash. The only way to escape the mishaps is to avoid the road, to remain stuck where we are, to build temporary shelters at wayside stations, and to determine to camp there until Jesus comes.

The life of a Christ follower is a narrow-road proposition, a continual journey forward, an adventure fraught with perils and pitfalls. Yet, breathtaking mountaintop views and heartachingly beautiful companionship are ours too, if we only keep our feet on the path and walk.

I'm only reminding you of what you're already aware. We can do everything right to prepare for a hard conversation and still it will go wrong. We can let down our guard, open our mouths and our hearts, only to find ourselves flat on our faces with our loving intentions crushed beneath someone else's boot.

Hard conversations always involve at least one other person, and we can't control that person (or, at least, we shouldn't). We can't decide how other people act, but we can decide the kind of person we are going to be.

God's Word asks us to choose to be like Jesus, to choose to be people who attempt the impossible, to love with our hearts, actions, and words in a world that chooses hate, as we further the kingdom of God.

ARTwork

Answer: Look back at the Scripture verses for unit 1, Ezekiel 3:10–11. With that Scripture in mind, how would you define success when it comes to having hard conversations?

Read: In Acts 15:36–40, we see a hard conversation that didn't end optimally for Paul and Barnabas. In Mark 10:17–22, Jesus's conversation with the rich young ruler doesn't end in what most of us would consider "success." What lesson can we glean from these two stories?

Try: Summarize. All conversational types benefit from clarifying others' points through summarizing (like reflection, only longer). Allow people to speak their minds. Then, before we respond, say, "Before I respond, I want to be sure I've understood you. If you don't mind, I'd like to try to summarize what you're saying and what you'd like to see happen because of our conversation. Then please correct me if I've misunderstood you." Some keys to making this effective follow:

- Use the other people's language as much as possible. When paraphrasing, it can be tempting to editorialize. (For example, "You're angry with me because it's totally unfair that someone your age should have a ridiculous curfew like ten p.m. when no one else you know has to be in that early." As opposed to "You're angry with me for exercising good parental judgment that other local parents aren't loving enough to do."
- Pay attention to body language as you summarize. If you've heard properly, you may observe them visibly relaxing and nodding their heads. If you've misunderstood, they will likely pull away, scowl, shake their heads, or make faces.
- Refrain from starting your own commentary with your body language, facial expressions, or tone of voice while you're summarizing. Don't allow sarcasm, anger, scorn, or frustration into your summary. Sincerely try to capture what they've said and what they hope will result from your conversation.

Give them time to correct any misunderstanding. Remember the others may not have prepared for this hard conversation the way you're learning to do. By summarizing before you respond, you assist them with knowing "What's your point?" Then you can respond to what they're saying, not a misinterpretation.

If we're worried our memory may be a barrier to summarizing, we may ask if they mind if we jot notes while they speak. Sometimes this reinforces how much we value listening and understanding them.

Lesson 2

Impossible Love

So we have come to know and to believe the love that
God has for us. God is love, and whoever abides in
love abides in God, and God abides in him.
(1 John 4:16)

L et's remember we're having these hard conversations as an act of love. In these days of abusers, users, addicts, enablers, entitled mindsets, and anti-Christian worldviews, even in these days, God refuses to release us from His command to love.

How are we supposed to do that? Seriously, most days we look like chumps. Smart money in these times is not on people who love. The point spread of this generation falls to those who keep up their guard, hold their affections close to their vests, invest love prudently in a chosen few who prove themselves capable of receiving love responsibly, and reciprocating by changing and loving in return.

We cannot love like God (although that is the call). He loves lavishly, extravagantly, with no thought to return. He loves with patience, kindness, humility, without demand, without irritability or resentment. His love is never rude.

God holds out a love that bears all things, believes all things, hopes all things, endures all things.

How are we supposed to love like that? That's a sitting-duck love. That's a love that gets taken for a ride. Love that gets taken for granted. Love that extends itself for those unable or unwilling to love in return.

People don't do that anymore. We're too smart for that kind of love in these times.

Of course, Jesus showed us what this love looks like. Jesus lived in this hard, Roman-army-ruled world full of thugs, murderers, scoffers, and jackboots. Jesus knew scoundrels, hypocrites, oppressors, and whores.

Jesus offered the gold standard of love to men who smelled like fish and women who reeked of perfume purchased by their adulteries.

Jesus was aware at their last Passover meal that only hours later, one of his closest disciples would betray Him, one would deny Him, and the rest would abandon Him. And yet, we read the words of John 13:1: "Now before the Feast of the Passover, when Jesus knew that his hour had come to depart out of this world to the Father, having loved his own who were in the world, he loved them to the end."

He saw, better than we, the depth of our sins, the blackness of our souls, and the perversion of our thoughts. Yet, He offered us love. Pure love. Heavenly love. Love divine, all loves excelling. Love that defines love. Jesus offered the gold standard of love to men who smelled like fish and women who reeked of perfume purchased by their adulteries, and He continues to offer it to us and our children.

He loved the ones who spit in His face, laughed at His captivity, crowned Him with thorns, and nailed Him to a tree. He loved under fire, under duress, under a captor's boot, and under a scorner's laugh. He loved when His Father said no to His prayers and when His dearest friends deserted Him in His darkest hour. He loved when He had to look on the pain in His mother's face as she watched Him die.

No one took advantage of Jesus—He offered His love freely (1 John 3). No one took His life—He laid His life down (John 10). He didn't love because anyone forced Him to love. He loved because He is love (1 John 4). He bore all things, believed all things, hoped all things, and endured all things (1 Cor. 13). And He still does.

So, God asks us to do the impossible—to love freely, as He loved, and to lay down our lives for our brothers, but He did it first, He did it best, and we can do it because He will make us able (John 14:12).

If you think about it, how we operate in this world comes down to one simple question: Would you rather be Charlie Brown or Lucy?

How can *Peanuts* characters teach us how to live out our call to bear all things, believe all things, hope all things, and endure all things? By always running to kick the football.

For over fifty years, Charles Schultz testified to us. Every fall, Lucy offered to hold the football for Charlie Brown to kick. Charlie Brown sometimes hesitated, but he always relented and went for the kick. Every single time, Lucy yanked the ball away, and Charlie flew through the air, landing flat on his back staring at the skies.

All of us who offer our love in these times know exactly how Charlie feels. The world abounds with Lucys. They seem like the smart ones in the moment of the fall. But what we must ask ourselves is this: At the end of the day, would we rather be Charlie Brown or Lucy?

We can join the smart ones who withhold their love, stay quiet, hide the truth in their breast pocket, smirk at Charlie's gullibility and hope, toy with and deceive for the pleasure of those who spectate, display their own arrogance and superiority through trickery, and refuse to really allow themselves to be children and engage in the real game.

Or we can bear all things, believe all things, hope all things, endure all things, and always, always choose to run and kick the ball. Of course, as we've discussed, there are times for safe boundaries, for limits, for silence, but we always hold out loving hope.

What choice will you make? Will you remain on the sidelines? Will you join the smug Lucy crowd? Or will you open your heart like Charlie and join the conversation?

Love speaks up. Love says challenging, true, eternal things. Love believes change is possible. Love engages in hard conversations.

ARTwork

Answer: How have you benefited from the love of Jesus Christ? In what ways does His love impact your life?

Read: What does 1 John 4:7–21 teach us about the relationship of our love for God and our love for others? Read John 16 and consider the trouble and the comfort Jesus promised His disciples in His last hours before the crucifixion. What truth can we apply to our attempts at hard conversations?

Try: Forewarned keeps people at the table. We sometimes falsely believe that to warn people of a hard conversation will cause them greater anxiety or inspire avoidance behavior, but often the opposite is true. In ministry with families, I'll often tell them, "Together, we're going to do hard things and face hard truths. But that's okay. Parents do hard things. That's part of the job." I normalize the work ahead. After a few weeks, some of them repeat this back to me: "I'm a parent. I do hard things."

It's also productive to state truth like this at the start of hard group conversations, when discipling others, or in conflict resolution: "We're here to discuss hard things and talk about stuff we'd all rather avoid discussing. There'll be moments we want to walk away from the table, but we're not going to do that because we love one another. God is here.

We're going to see this through. Hebrews 10:39 says, 'But we are not of those who shrink back and are destroyed, but of those who have faith and preserve their souls.' This, loved ones, is us."

All We Need

His divine power has granted to us all things that pertain to life and godliness, through the knowledge of him who called us to his own glory and excellence. (2 Peter 1:3)

God promises in 2 Peter 1:3 that He has given us all we need for life and godliness. We do, in fact and faith, have all we need to do whatever God sets before us. Hawks, turtles, and chameleons are capable, in Christ, of navigating hard conversations.

Even when words pale against situations. Even at times when we think a conversation will absolutely break our hearts.

My family filled the emergency room cubicle, surrounding my father, who moaned in agony. He and mom had just experienced the worst summer. Mom's car was hit by a tractor trailer, and she was still recovering. They'd said goodbye to their much-loved dog. And now, my father had fallen down a flight of stairs, resulting in a fractured spine.

We'd all taken turns beside his gurney as we awaited test results. Now it was mine.

"I'm so sorry this happened," he moaned. "I can't breathe. I don't want this to be happening." He looked so fragile, so agonized. Not like the take-charge fire chief I'd known my whole life. Two years earlier, he'd been given six months to live, but he'd made drastic life changes to regain his health. Now this. I wondered if people ever actually explode from stress.

I stroked his hand. Dad struggled to breathe. The nurse had already explained that was from pain and anxiety. Uncharacteristically panicked, he said quietly, "I don't know what this is. What is this feeling? I can handle pain. I can't live with this."

"Dad, you're overwhelmed. We don't know what happens next, but you won't always feel this way." I inhaled, calming myself. "This feeling will go away, probably in the days to come, but right now, anxiety is perfectly normal. You're used to being in control. That will come back, but right now, we just have to go through this. There's nothing any of us can do to change it. It's unfair, but this just is. We're here with you, though."

Words have never felt as useless as they did in that moment. They didn't ease his pain or calm his fears. They didn't roll back time to the moment before his fall. They didn't make him a better candidate for the high-risk surgery to come or the weeks in rehab.

But Dad knew he wasn't alone, and during the ordeal, sometimes he would say, "I won't always feel like this, right?" So, I knew he'd heard us. Our words felt useless, but they weren't, not in the hands of our great God.

The man who was once functionally comatose to his family now lay surrounded by loved ones who couldn't imagine the world without him. That didn't happen without God, prayer, and a host of hard conversations. As unbearable as it was, that crowded emergency room cubicle testified to the power of God to transform, to heal, and to redeem.

My friends didn't know what they were doing over coffee that night years ago, but they stuck with me. I had no idea what I was doing as my father faced his greatest challenge. All I wanted to do was run, but by God's grace I stayed.

> **Showing up gives God the opportunity to include us in what He's doing, and that is worth every moment of uncertainty and pain.**

With all the hard conversations I've had through the years, each new one presents its own unique challenge and I feel like a novice again, wondering what I'm going to say this time.

This will likely be your experience too.

Still, showing up gives God the opportunity to include us in what He's doing, and that is worth every moment of uncertainty and pain.

Embed your life with Christ. Immerse yourself in His Word. Allow Him to expand your ability to love. Practice the tools in this book and prepare for the conversations you can see coming.

When you're in them, inhale, then exhale. Remember you're not alone. Make eye contact. Ask questions and then listen to the answers. Be gentle. Be humble. Be truthful. Be real. Set boundaries. Offer kindness and respect. Love with an open heart. Open your mouth, and let words come out.

Words aren't nothing. At the end of the day, hard conversations are a way to be present with somebody in the middle of something that person must go through or get through.

Our God spoke the world into being. Jesus is the Living Word. Words are powerful weapons against deception. Words are a beautiful vehicle for grace. Words are catalysts for repentance and transformation. Words are a channel for love. Having hard conversations is a way of being like Jesus.

As I've said from the opening pages, hard conversations are an art. They require practice, effort, and grace. They're also a sacred art, a calling by Christ on our lives, a kingdom-building work He compels us and equips us to do. Speaking truth is one way we invoke Jesus into our everyday and represent Him even in the everyday.

Our studio is all around us. We're ready. Let's commence conversations.

ARTWORK

Answer: What motivates your interest in hard conversations?

Read: Galatians 6:1–10 is a wonderful passage about interacting with other believers. How can a hard conversation be a way of putting verse 10 into action?

Try: "What is your understanding of what is happening?" "What do you know about what's going on?" These two questions are extremely useful when opening a conversation with the very young or the very old.

Sometimes we forget what it's like to be children and how much we actually understand before anyone tells us. And until we arrive in our senior years, we don't have significant understanding about that. So, when we open hard conversations with children or with seniors, it's good practice to ask them first what they already understand about a situation.

When I was a child, my father was hospitalized after a fire to be treated for smoke inhalation. Those were the days when no one explained anything to children, so we worked out the details on our own.

Imagine my parents' horror when they were called into the school principal's office. My young brother had informed his friends that the doctors had cut off our father's head, allowed the smoke to escape, and then sewn it back on Frankenstein style. Sometimes a few details make all the difference.

It may sound like this.

"Abbie, you know Mommy's been going to a lot of doctor visits and now she's in the hospital. Have you heard anyone talking about what's happening?"

"I heard Aunt Sadie say she might not come home from the hospital. Does Mommy like it there better than she likes it here?"

"No, Mommy wishes she was home, not at the hospital. Do you know why people stay in hospitals?"

"So that doctors can take care of them and make them better."

"That's right. Mommy's sick and the doctors are trying to make her better. Sometimes, though, everything the doctors do doesn't make people better."

"Like Grandma? When the doctors couldn't make Grandma better, she went to live with Jesus. Is Mommy going to live with Jesus too?"

By asking questions throughout the conversation, we learn how the child is processing the information and what misperceptions (or sometimes some spot-on perceptions) he or she may have.

This is also useful with seniors who are often way ahead of us with their insight, but sometimes are foggier than we realize: "Mom, what did you hear the doctor saying about your prognosis?" or "Dad, you know I've been stressed at work lately. Do you know any more details about what I'm going through?" are great ways to know where your conversation is starting while respecting that they may understand more than you realize.

HEART OF THE ART PRACTICE

Read Psalms 107 and 136, which speak to God's enduring love in all circumstances. God knows that recalling our history of successes inspires future faith. The Israelites made a habit of singing about victories and recording the many kindnesses of God in psalms. As we learn to have hard conversations, we make mistakes, suffer hurts, and stumble, but we also grow, gain victories, and witness God at work. Begin your own list of hard conversations that had positive results. Keep it handy and add to it as you remain open to having more. May God guide us into all love and truth by the grace and mercy of Jesus Christ until we arrive safely home.

Go on, now. Let's start talking.

AN INVITATION TO KEEP TALKING

I don't want our conversation to end here. If you'd like to stay connected, drop by my website at loriroeleveld.com and subscribe or link to me through social media. I've developed a variety of workshops on *The Art of Hard Conversations*. Contact me through the speaking page of my website to discuss the needs of your group.

Courage! The adventure is upon us, friend. Come find me. I'll be looking for you.